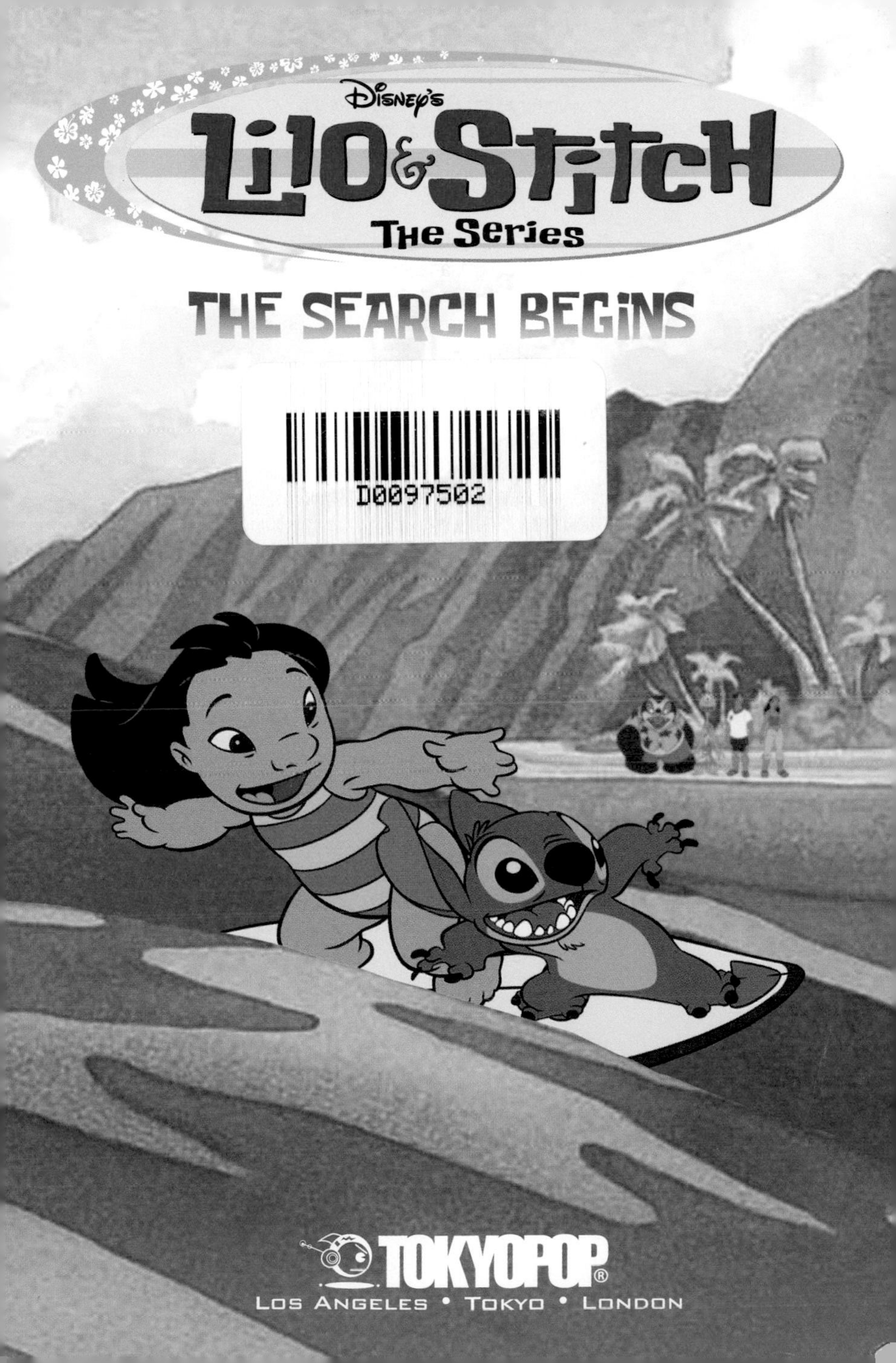
Disney's
Lilo & Stitch
The Series
THE SEARCH BEGINS
TOKYOPOP®
LOS ANGELES • TOKYO • LONDON

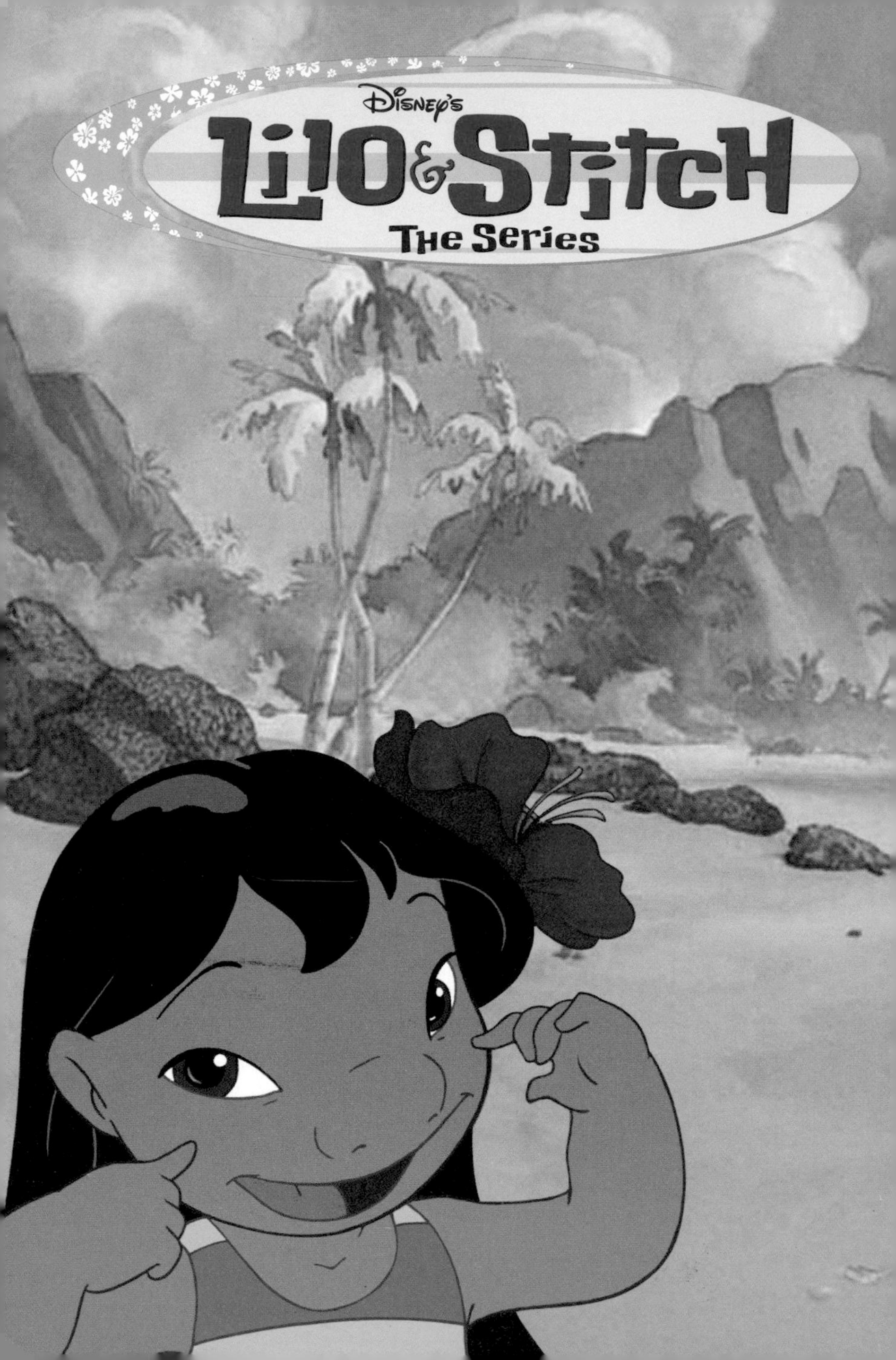
Disney's
Lilo & Stitch
The Series

Disney's

Lilo & Stitch

The Series

THE SEARCH BEGINS

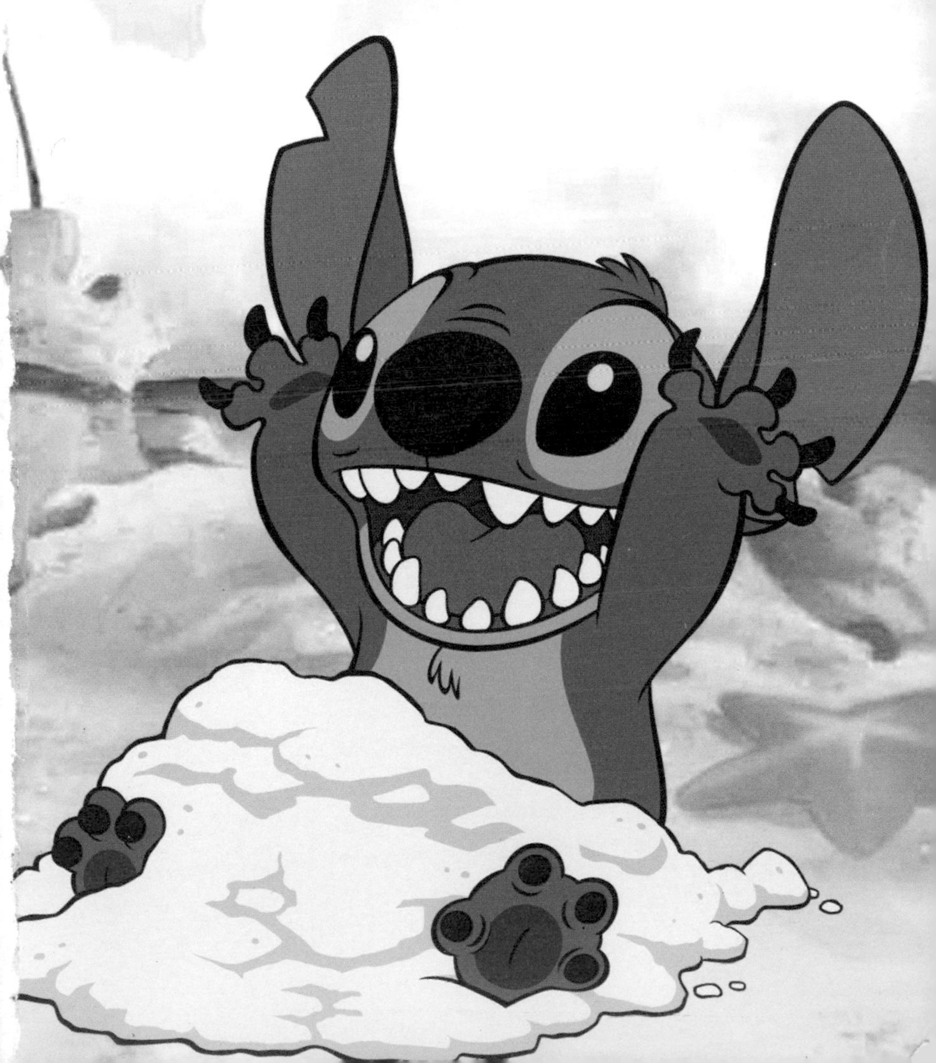

Contributing Editor - Tim Beedle
Graphic Design & Lettering - Jennifer Nunn-Iwai, Tomás Montalvo-Lagos, & Yolanda Petriz
Graphic Artists - Jennifer Nunn-Iwai & Tomás Montalvo-Lagos
Cover Layout - Aaron Suhr

Editors - Elizabeth Hurchalla & Jod Kaftan
Digital Imaging Manager - Chris Buford
Pre-Press Manager - Antonio DePietro
Production Managers - Jennifer Miller, Mutsumi Miyazaki
Art Director - Matt Alford
Managing Editor - Jill Freshney
VP of Production - Ron Klamert
President & C.O.O. - John Parker
Publisher & C.E.O. - Stuart Levy

E-mail: info@tokyopop.com
Come visit us online at www.TOKYOPOP.com

A TOKYOPOP® Cine-Manga® Book
TOKYOPOP Inc.
5900 Wilshire Blvd., Suite 2000, Los Angeles, CA 90036

Lilo & Stitch The Series
© 2004 Disney Enterprises, Inc.

ISBN: 1-59532-067-9

First TOKYOPOP® printing: June 2004

10 9 8 7 6 5 4 3 2

Printed in the USA

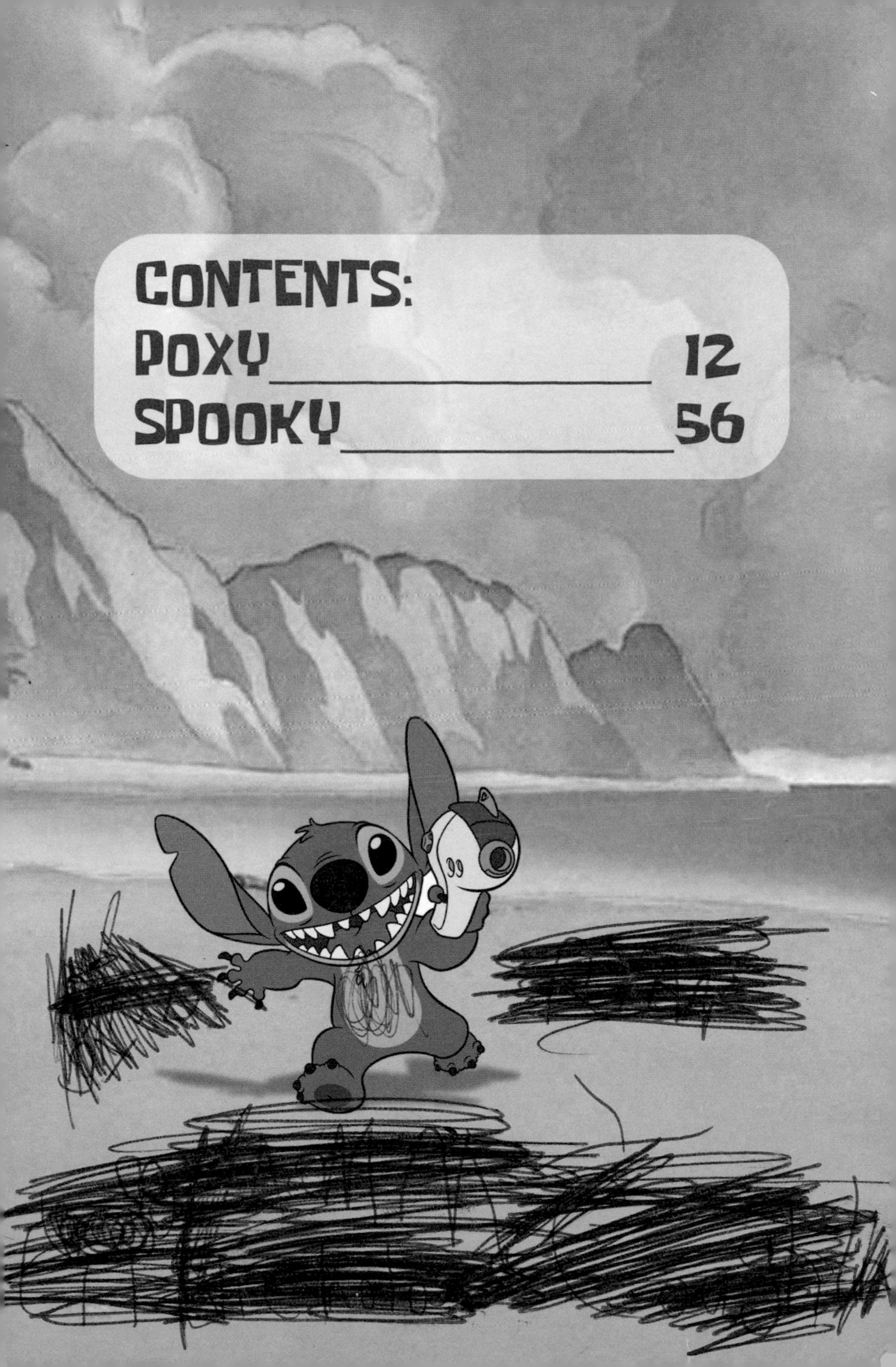

CONTENTS:

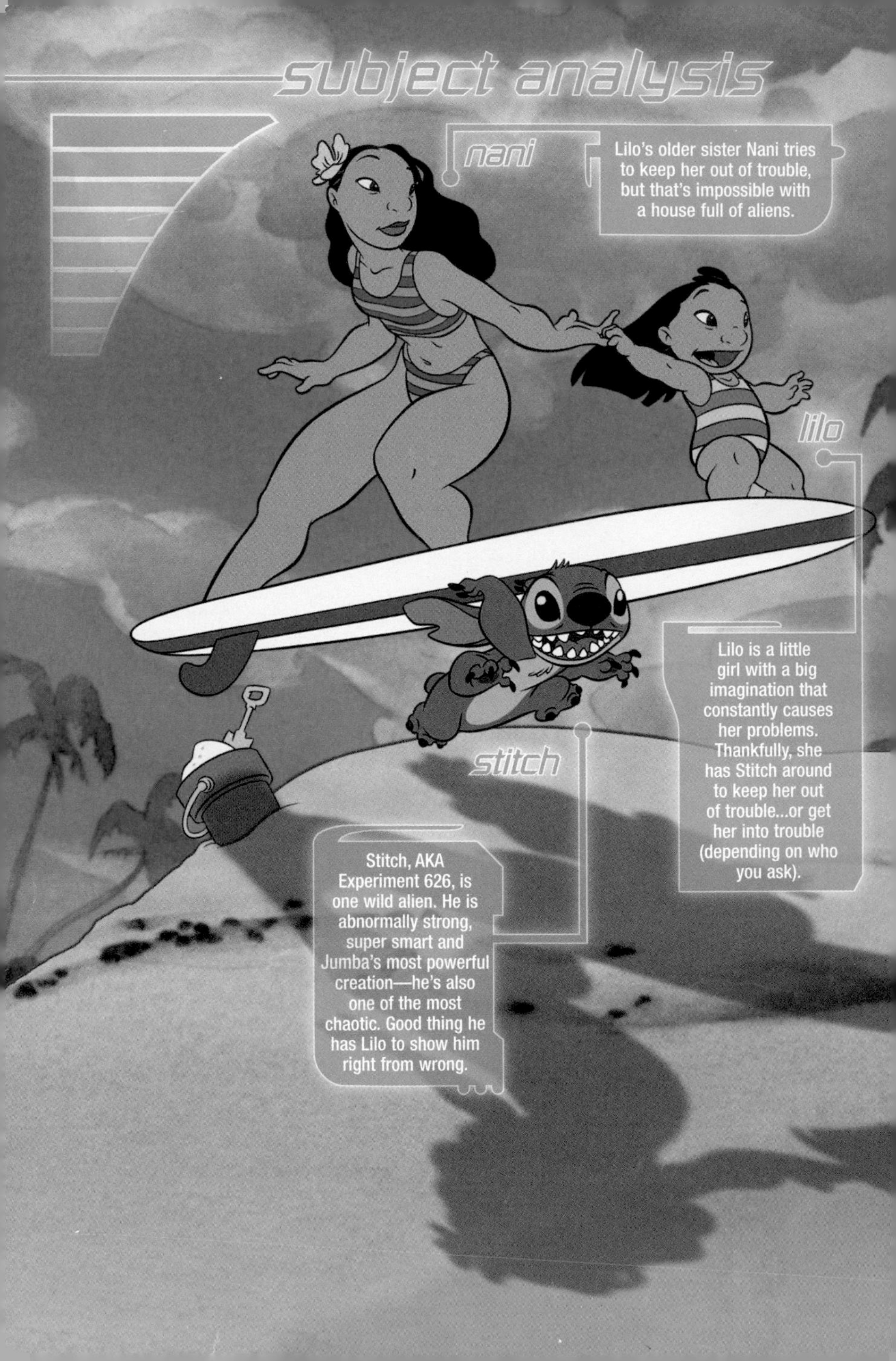
subject analysis
nani
Lilo's older sister Nani tries to keep her out of trouble, but that's impossible with a house full of aliens.
lilo
Lilo is a little girl with a big imagination that constantly causes her problems. Thankfully, she has Stitch around to keep her out of trouble...or get her into trouble (depending on who you ask).
stitch
Stitch, AKA Experiment 626, is one wild alien. He is abnormally strong, super smart and Jumba's most powerful creation—he's also one of the most chaotic. Good thing he has Lilo to show him right from wrong.

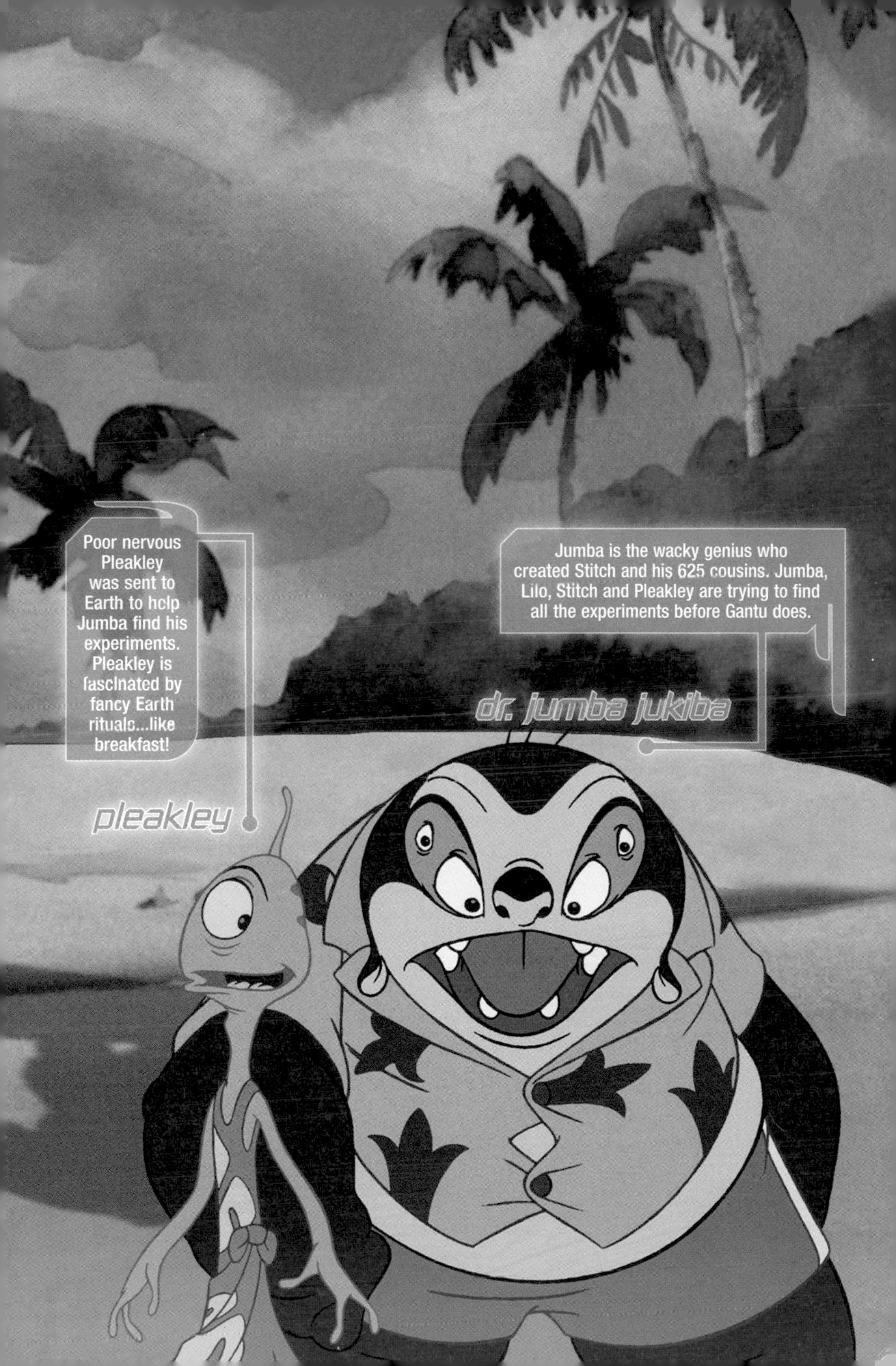
Poor nervous Pleakley was sent to Earth to help Jumba find his experiments. Pleakley is fascinated by fancy Earth rituals...like breakfast!
pleakley
Jumba is the wacky genius who created Stitch and his 625 cousins. Jumba, Lilo, Stitch and Pleakley are trying to find all the experiments before Gantu does.
dr. jumba jukiba

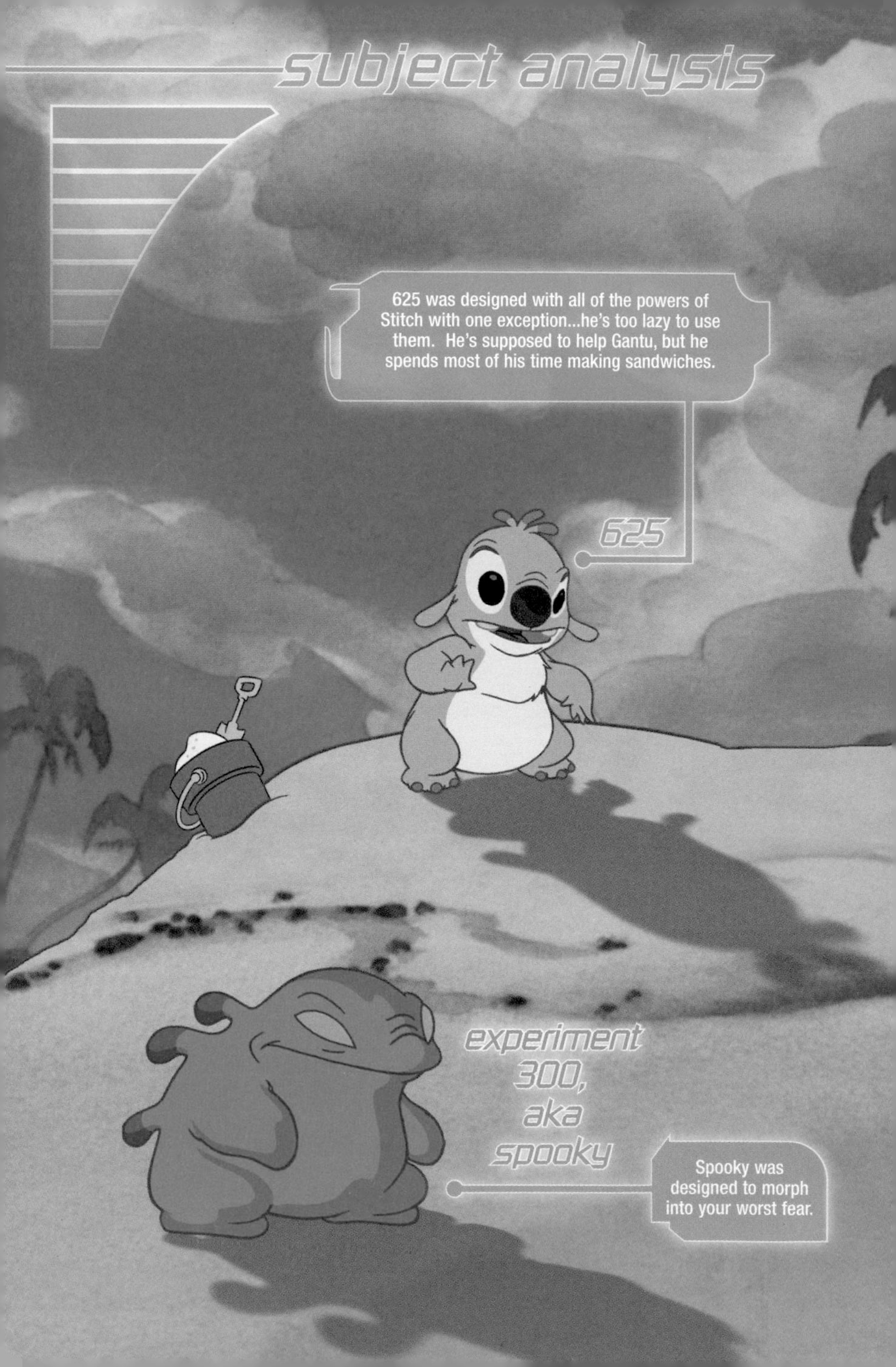
subject analysis
625 was designed with all of the powers of Stitch with one exception...he's too lazy to use them. He's supposed to help Gantu, but he spends most of his time making sandwiches.
625
experiment 300, aka spooky
Spooky was designed to morph into your worst fear.

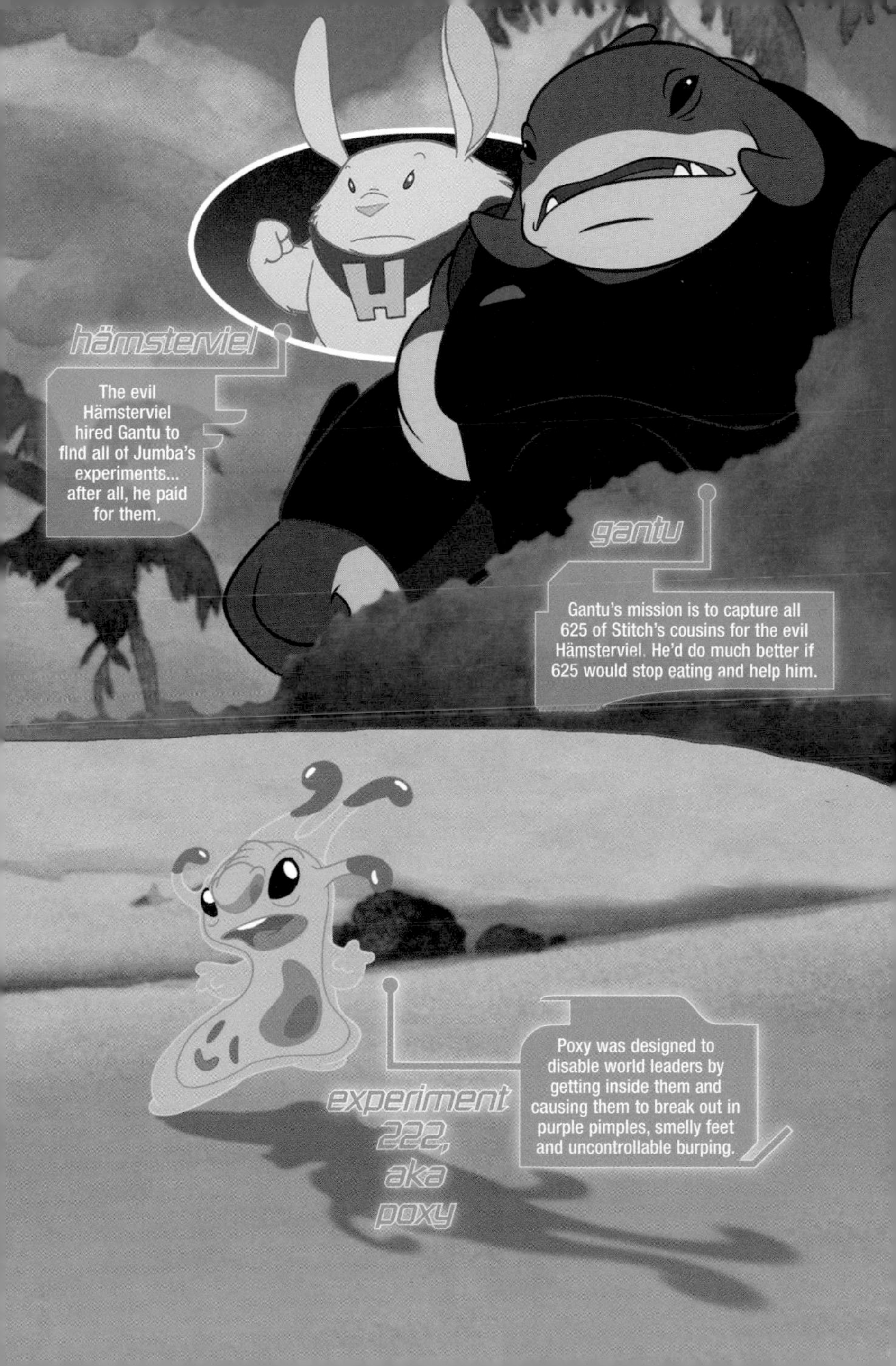
hämsterviel
The evil Hämsterviel hired Gantu to find all of Jumba's experiments... after all, he paid for them.
gantu
Gantu's mission is to capture all 625 of Stitch's cousins for the evil Hämsterviel. He'd do much better if 625 would stop eating and help him.
experiment 222, aka poxy
Poxy was designed to disable world leaders by getting inside them and causing them to break out in purple pimples, smelly feet and uncontrollable burping.

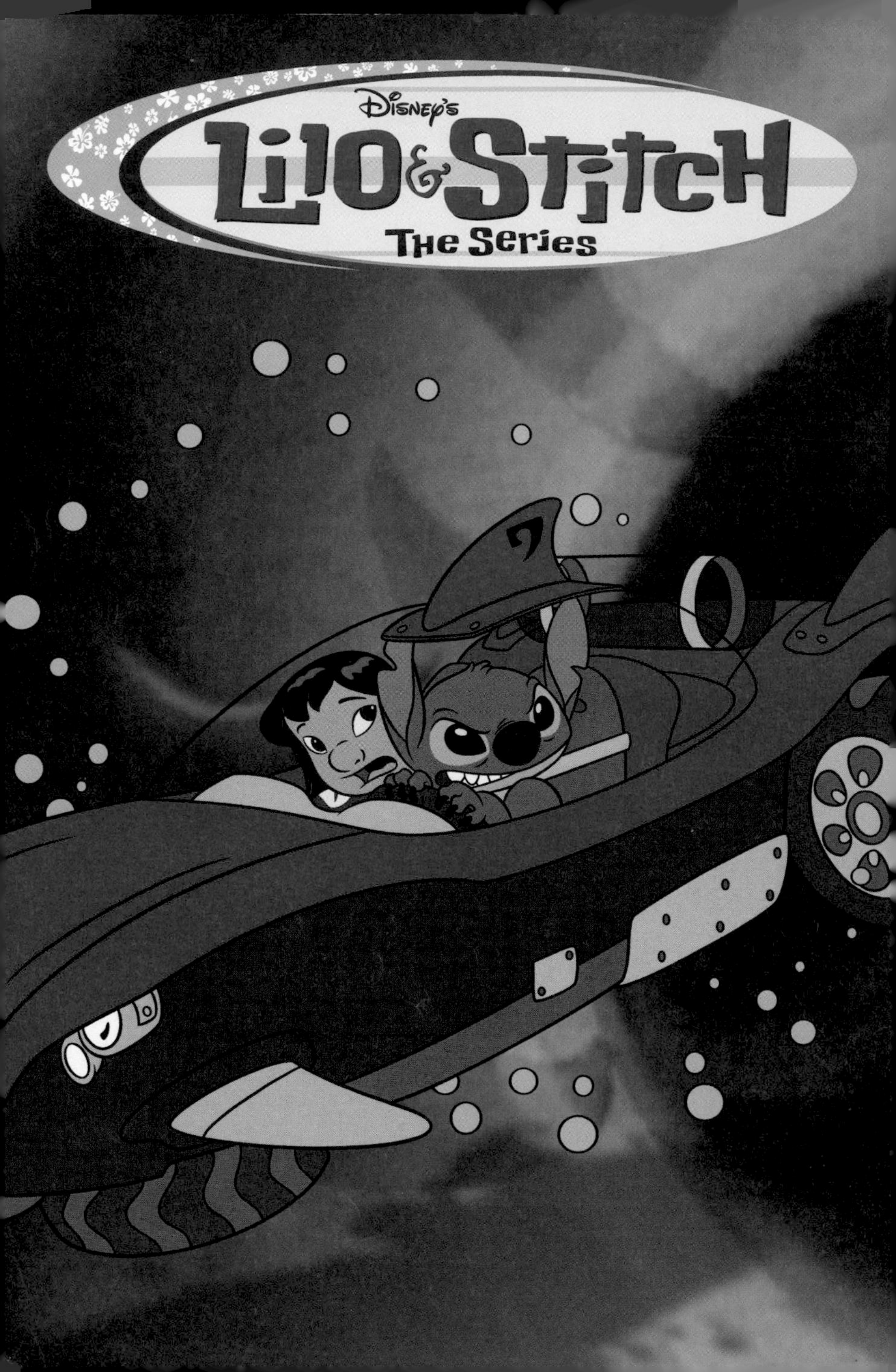
Disney's
Lilo & Stitch
The Series

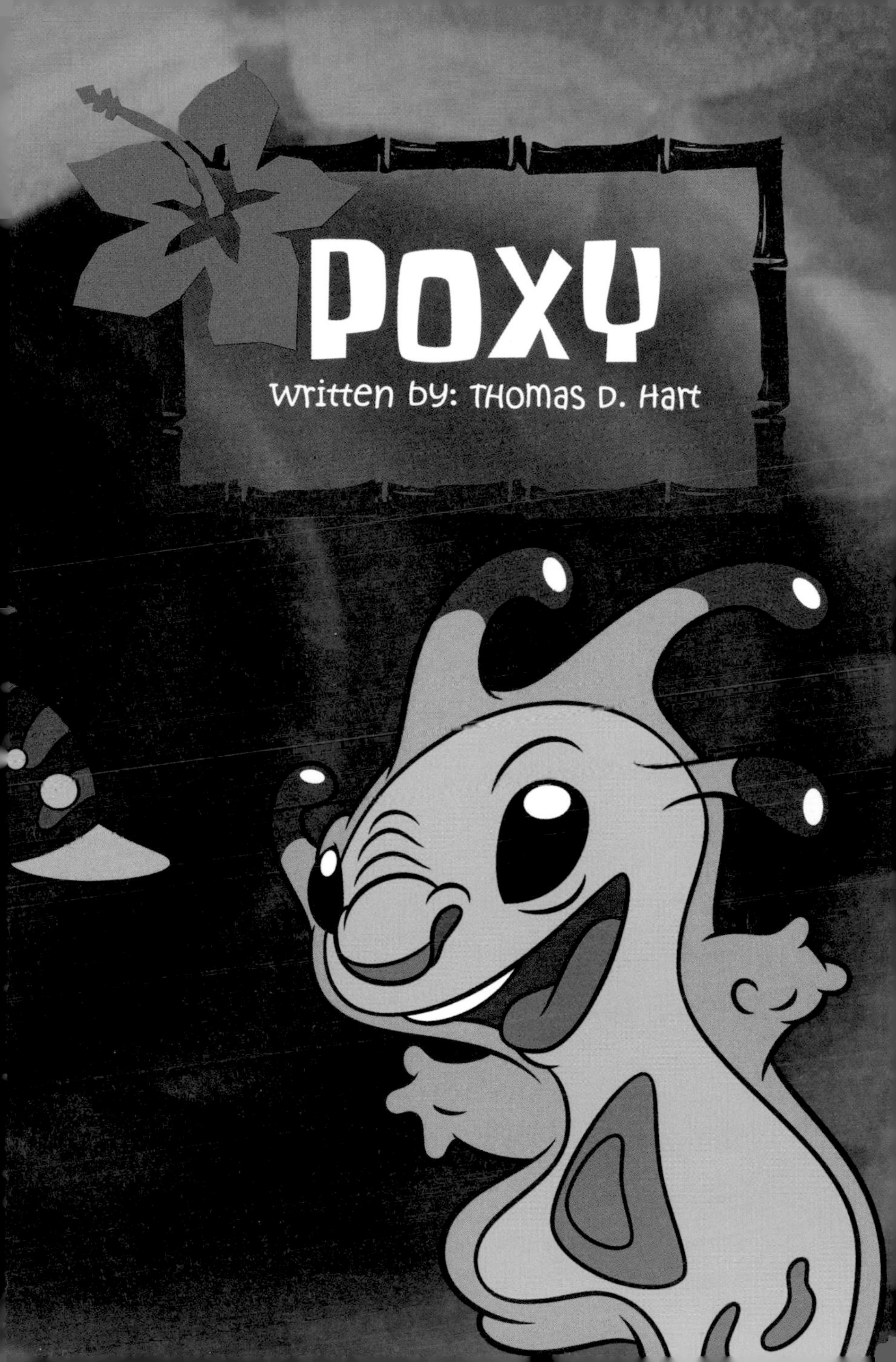
POXY
Written by: Thomas D. Hart

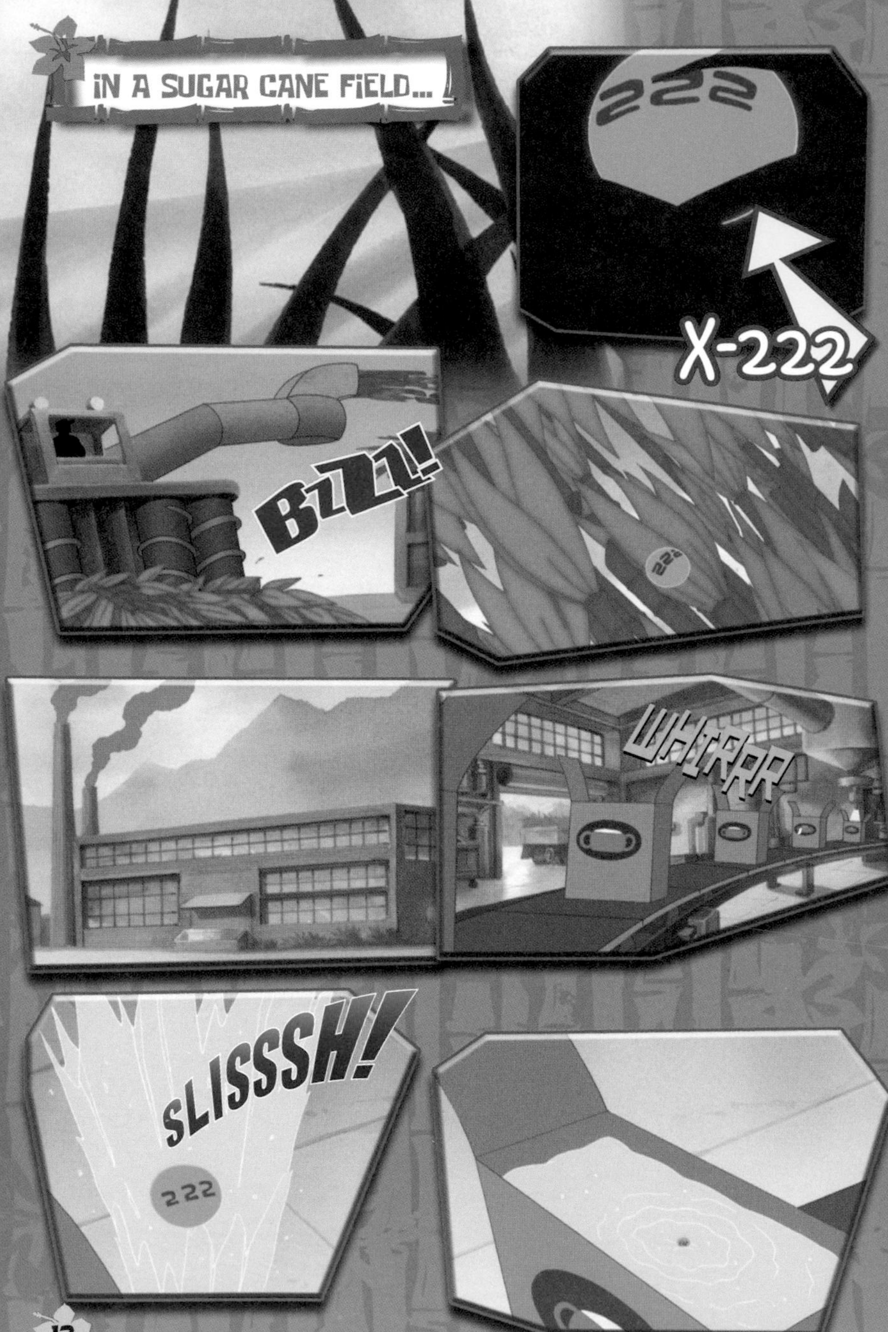
IN A SUGAR CANE FIELD...
222
X-222
BZZZ!
222
WHIRRR
SLISSSH!
222

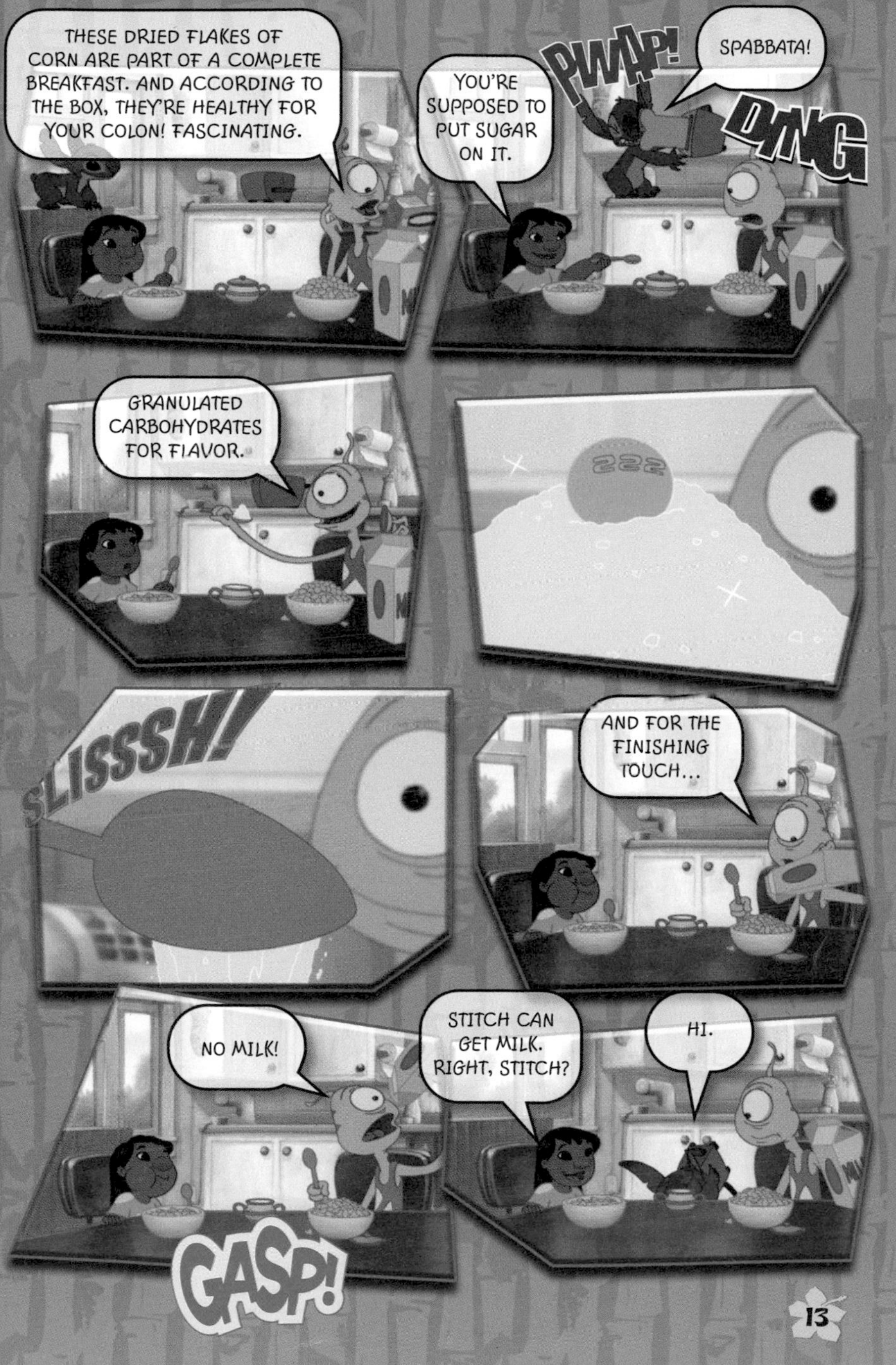
THESE DRIED FLAKES OF CORN ARE PART OF A COMPLETE BREAKFAST. AND ACCORDING TO THE BOX, THEY'RE HEALTHY FOR YOUR COLON! FASCINATING.
YOU'RE SUPPOSED TO PUT SUGAR ON IT.
PWAP!
SPABBATA!
DING
GRANULATED CARBOHYDRATES FOR FlAVOR.
222
SLISSSH!
AND FOR THE FINISHING TOUCH...
NO MILK!
GASP!
STITCH CAN GET MILK. RIGHT, STITCH?
HI.

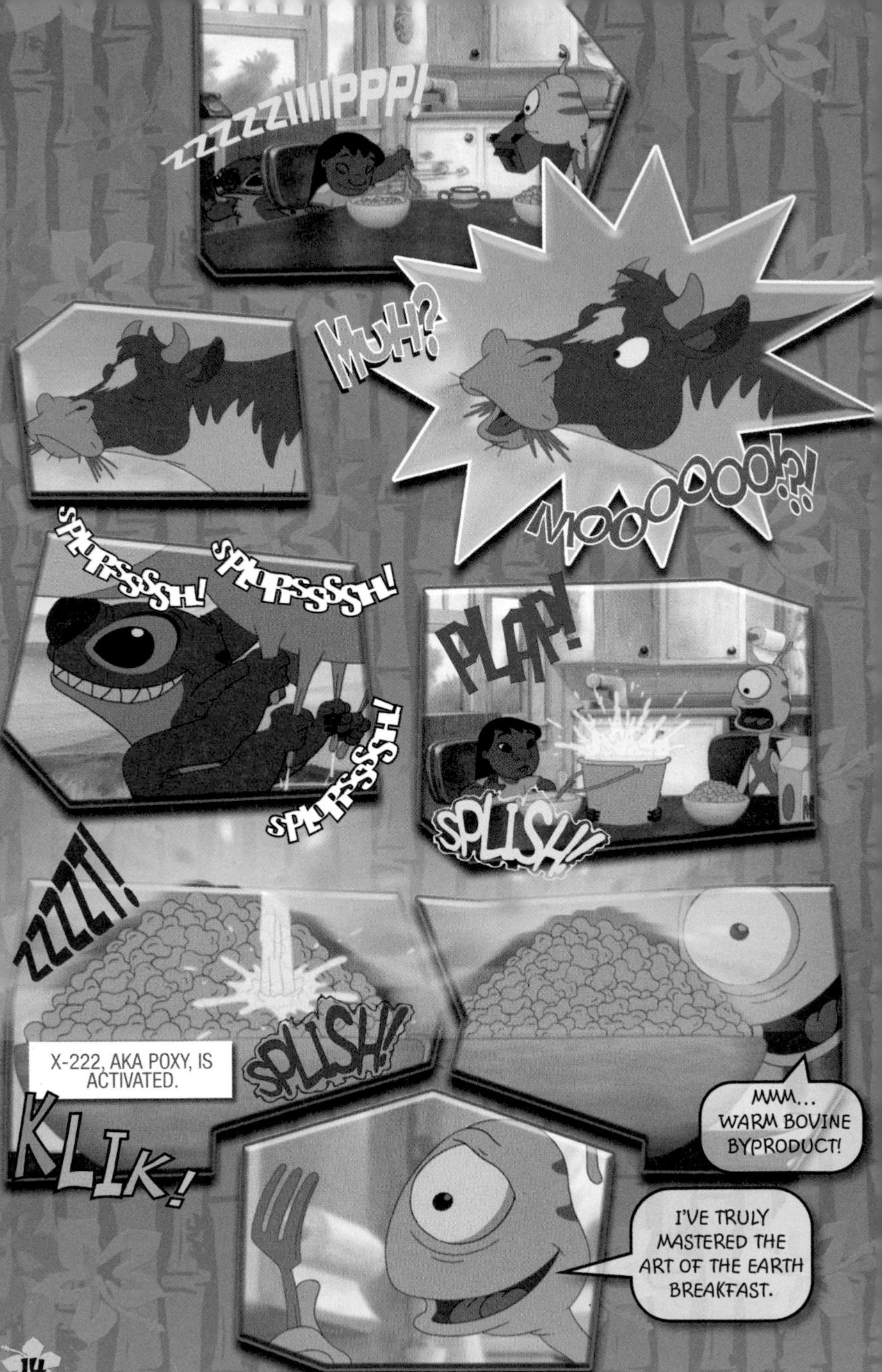
ZZZZZIIIIIPPP!
MUH?
MOOOOOOO!?!
SPLORSSSSH!
SPLORSSSSH!
SPLORSSSSH!
PLAP!
SPLISH!!
ZZZZT!
SPLISH!
X-222, AKA POXY, IS ACTIVATED.
KLIK!
MMM... WARM BOVINE BYPRODUCT!
I'VE TRULY MASTERED THE ART OF THE EARTH BREAKFAST.

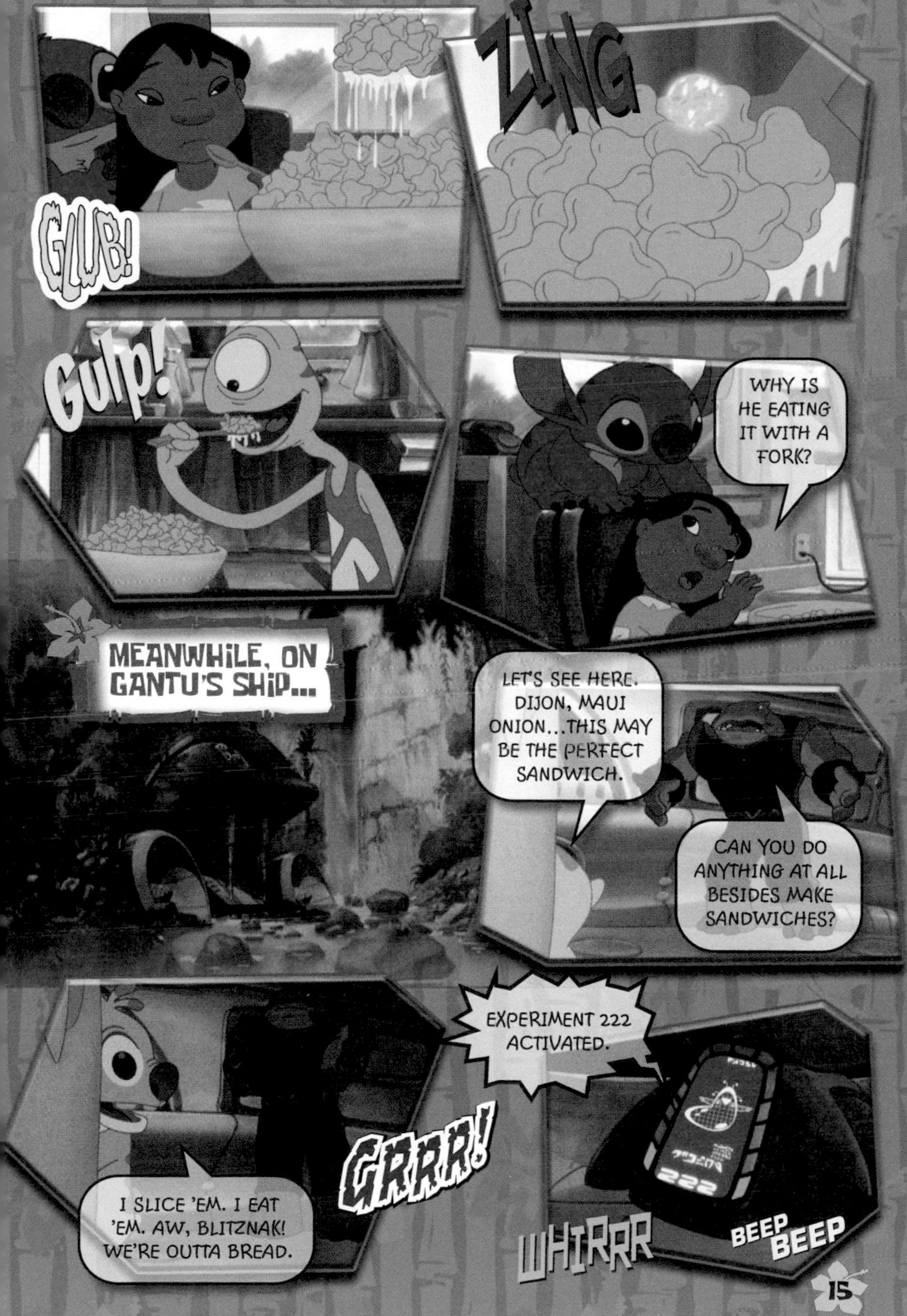
GLUB!
ZING
GULP!
WHY IS HE EATING IT WITH A FORK?
MEANWHILE, ON GANTU'S SHIP...
LET'S SEE HERE. DIJON, MAUI ONION...THIS MAY BE THE PERFECT SANDWICH.
CAN YOU DO ANYTHING AT ALL BESIDES MAKE SANDWICHES?
I SLICE 'EM. I EAT 'EM. AW, BLITZNAK! WE'RE OUTTA BREAD.
GRRR!
EXPERIMENT 222 ACTIVATED.
222
WHIRRR
BEEP BEEP

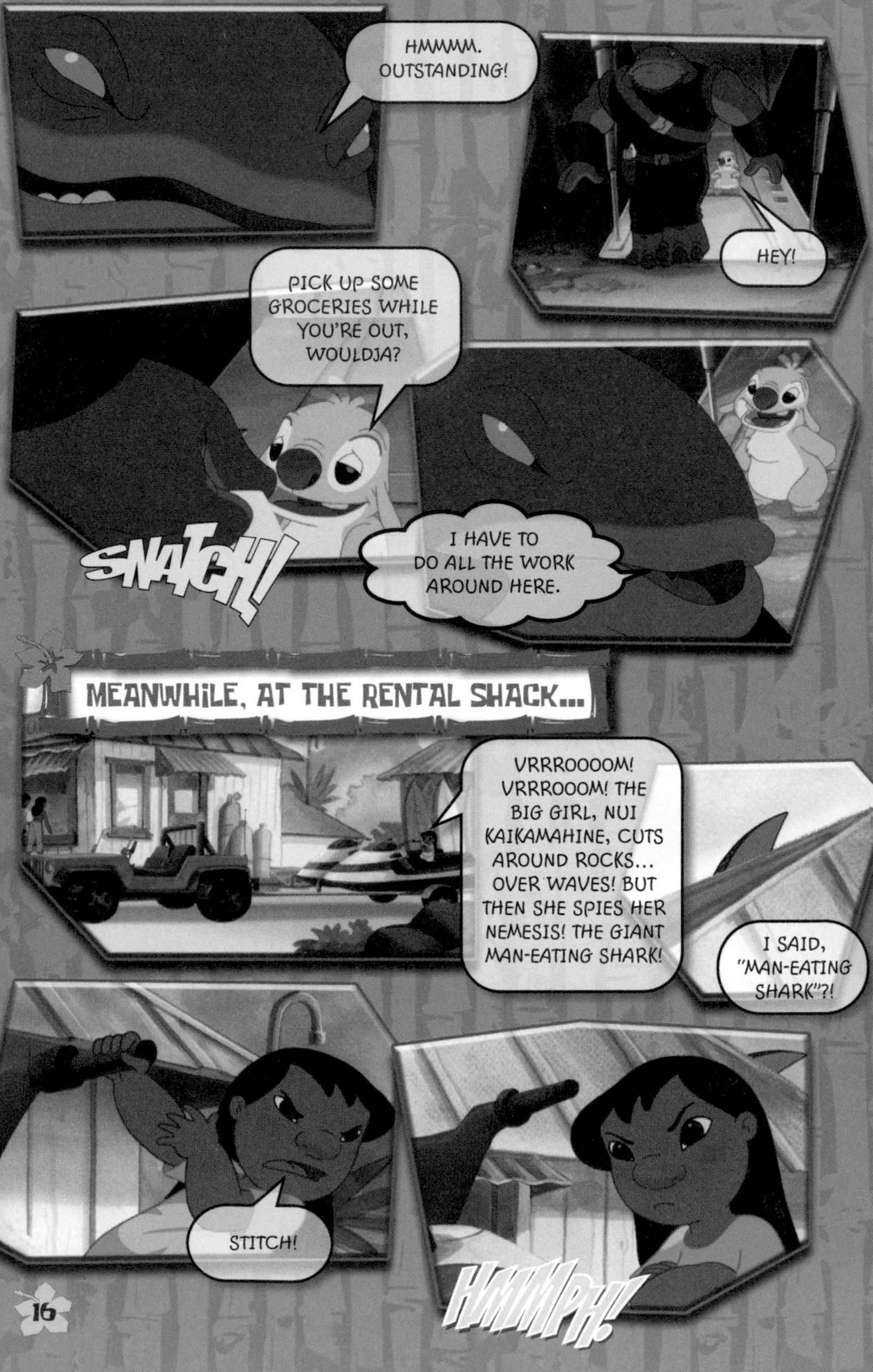
HMMMM. OUTSTANDING!
HEY!
PICK UP SOME GROCERIES WHILE YOU'RE OUT, WOULDJA?
SNATCH!
I HAVE TO DO ALL THE WORK AROUND HERE.
MEANWHILE, AT THE RENTAL SHACK...
VRRROOOOM! VRRROOOM! THE BIG GIRL, NUI KAIKAMAHINE, CUTS AROUND ROCKS... OVER WAVES! BUT THEN SHE SPIES HER NEMESIS! THE GIANT MAN-EATING SHARK!
I SAID, "MAN-EATING SHARK"?!
STITCH!
HMMPH!

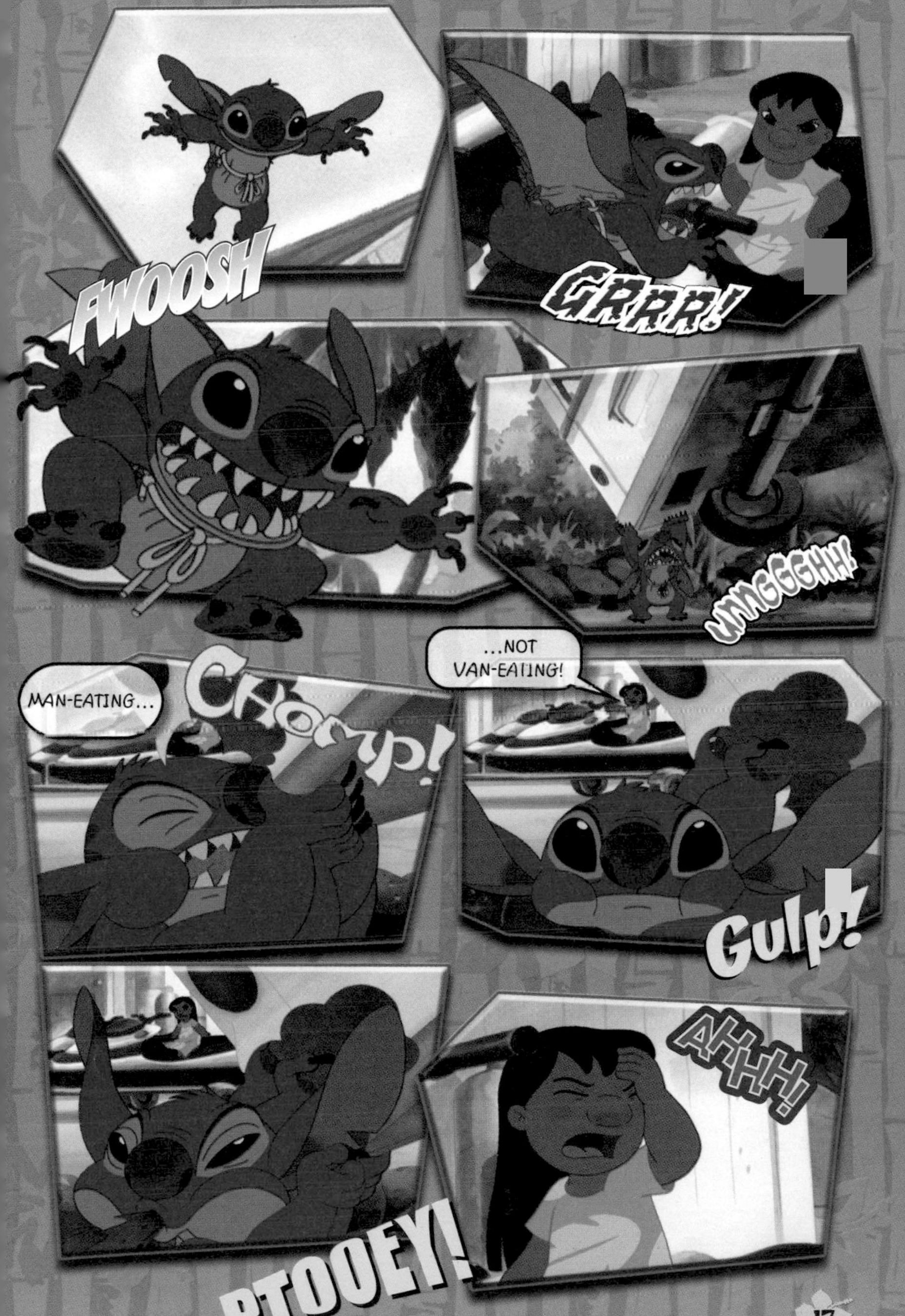
FWOOSH
GRRR!
UNNGGGHH!
MAN-EATING...
Chomp!
...NOT VAN-EATING!
Gulp!
PTOOEY!
AHHH!

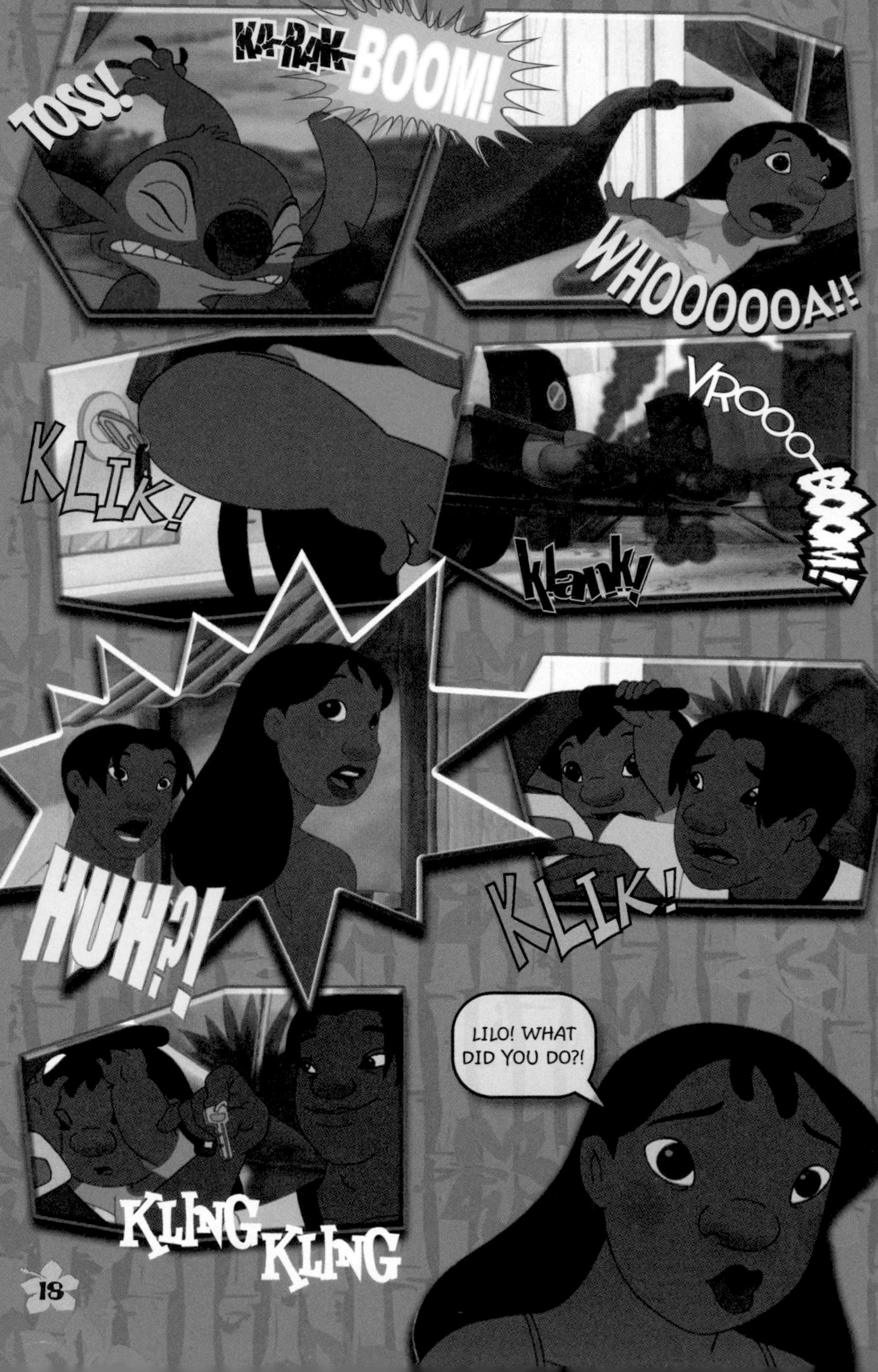
TOSS!
KA-RAK-BOOM!
WHOOOOOA!!
KLIK!
VROOO-BOOM!
KLANK!
HUH?!
KLIK!
KLING KLING
LILO! WHAT DID YOU DO?!

I THINK THIS ONE'S BROKE. YOU SHOULD TAKE BETTER CARE OF YOUR EQUIPMENT. I COULDA GOT HURT.

RUMMMBBBLE!

WHOOOOOA!!

FWUMP!

GRRRRR!

CHUPPY-CHEEPA!

THIS IS GOING TO NEED REPAIRS. BUT WE STILL HAVE ONE GOOD ONE.

I WANT TO GO WAVE RIDING TOO! CAN I COME? PLEEEEEEEAAAASSSEE?

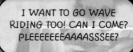

NOT UNTIL YOU'RE BIGGER.

BUT I DON'T GET INTO TROUBLE... TROUBLE GETS INTO ME!

WE'LL TALK LATER. AT HOME.

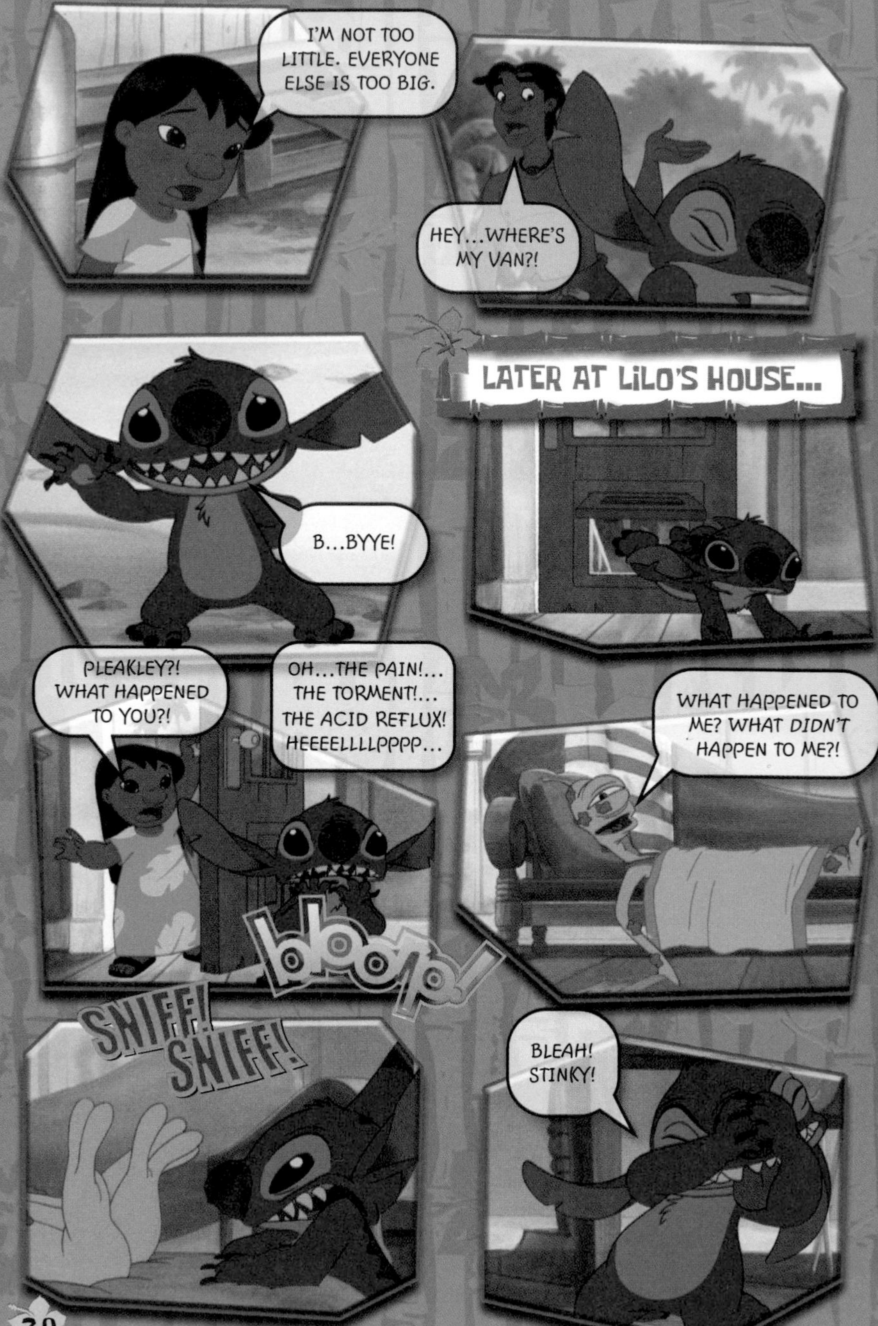
I'M NOT TOO LITTLE. EVERYONE ELSE IS TOO BIG.
HEY...WHERE'S MY VAN?!
B...BYYE!
LATER AT LILO'S HOUSE...
PLEAKLEY?! WHAT HAPPENED TO YOU?!
OH...THE PAIN!... THE TORMENT!... THE ACID REFLUX! HEEEELLLLPPPP...
bloop!
WHAT HAPPENED TO ME? WHAT *DIDN'T* HAPPEN TO ME?!
SNIFF! SNIFF!
BLEAH! STINKY!

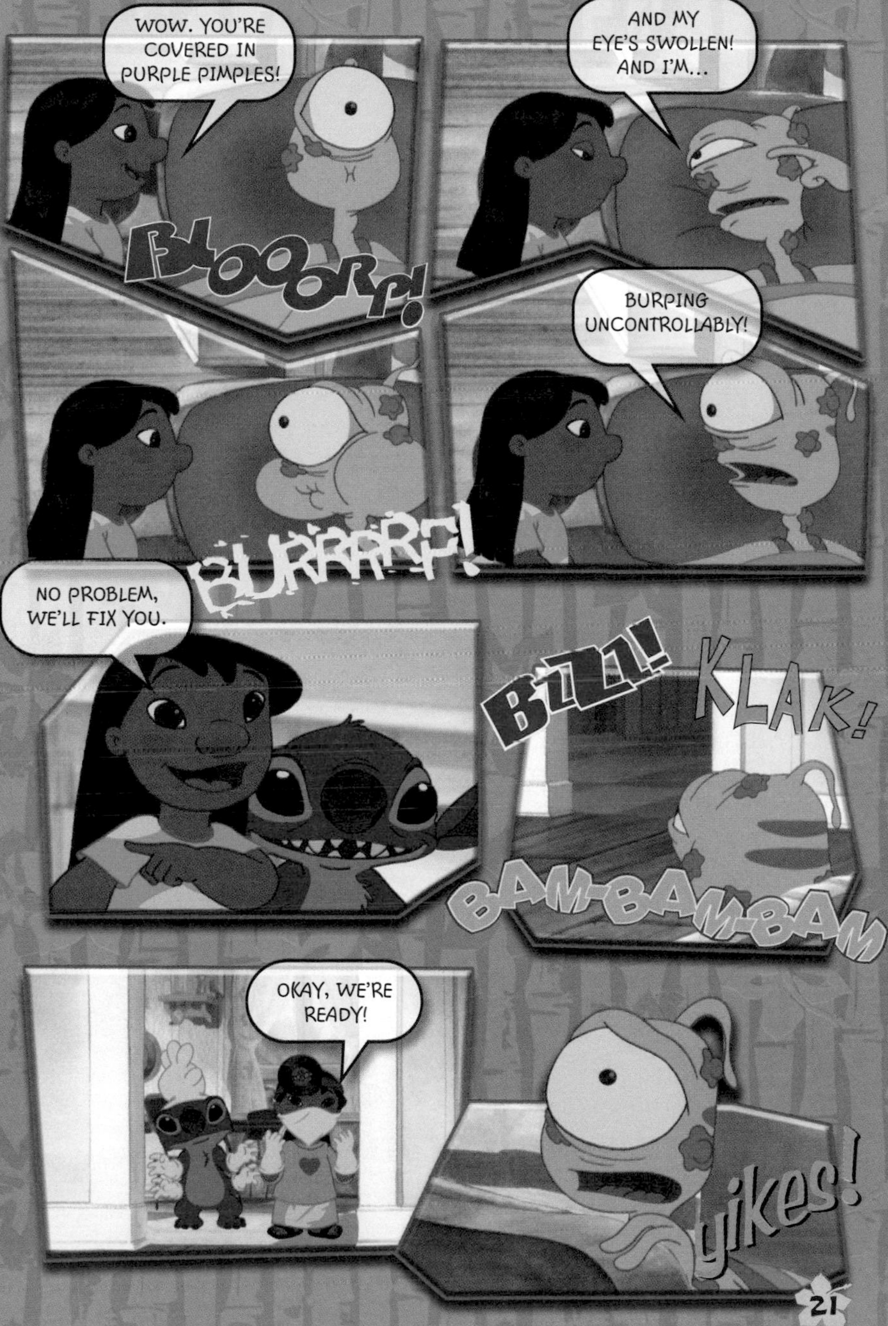
WOW. YOU'RE COVERED IN PURPLE PIMPLES!
AND MY EYE'S SWOLLEN! AND I'M...
BLOOORP!
BURPING UNCONTROLLABLY!
BURRRRP!
NO PROBLEM, WE'LL FIX YOU.
BZZZT!
KLAK!
BAM-BAM-BAM
OKAY, WE'RE READY!
yikes!

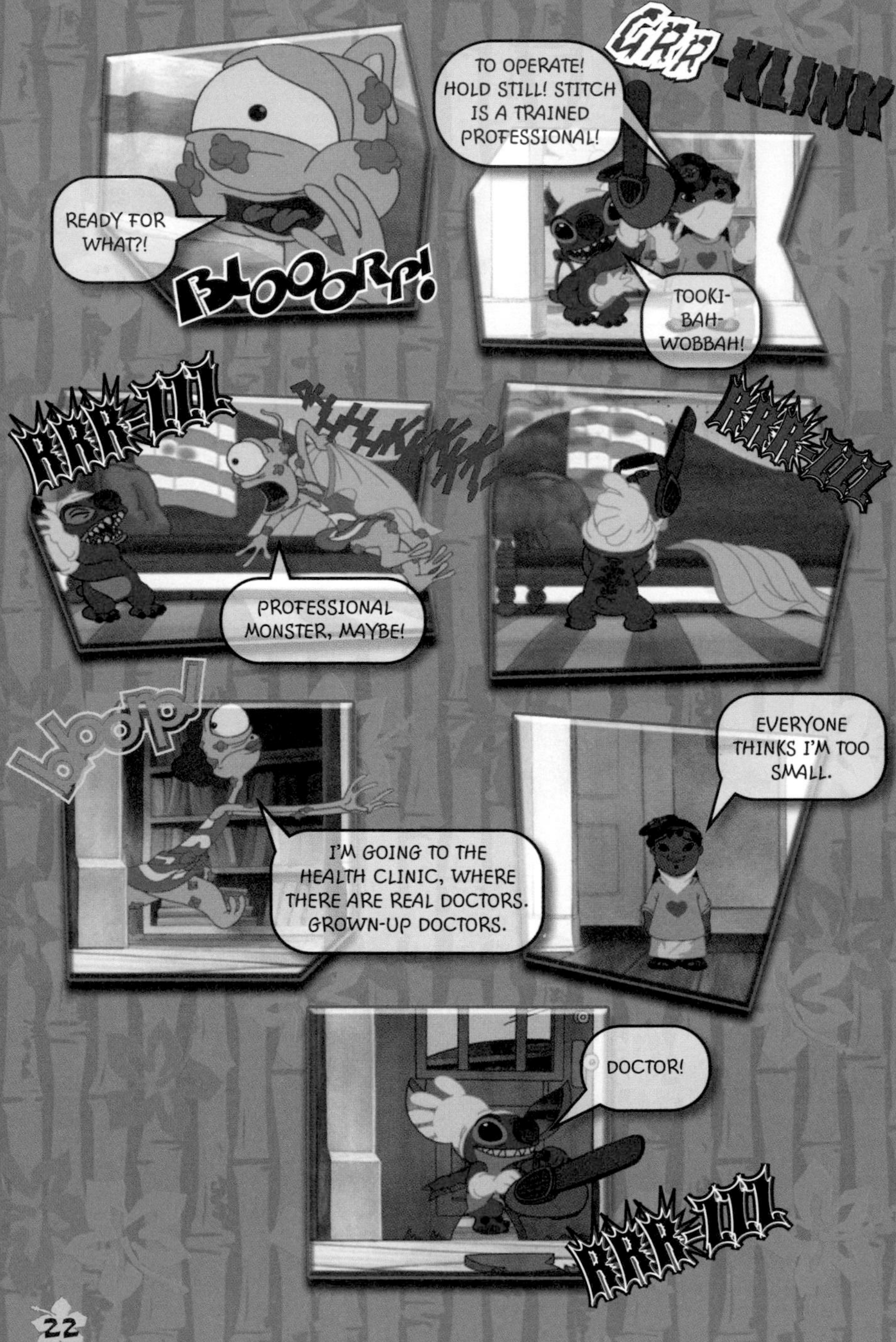
READY FOR WHAT?!
BLOOORP!
TO OPERATE! HOLD STILL! STITCH IS A TRAINED PROFESSIONAL!
GRR-KLINK
TOOKI-BAH-WOBBAH!
RRR-OOO
PROFESSIONAL MONSTER, MAYBE!
RRR-OOO
bloorp!
I'M GOING TO THE HEALTH CLINIC, WHERE THERE ARE REAL DOCTORS. GROWN-UP DOCTORS.
EVERYONE THINKS I'M TOO SMALL.
DOCTOR!
RRR-OOO

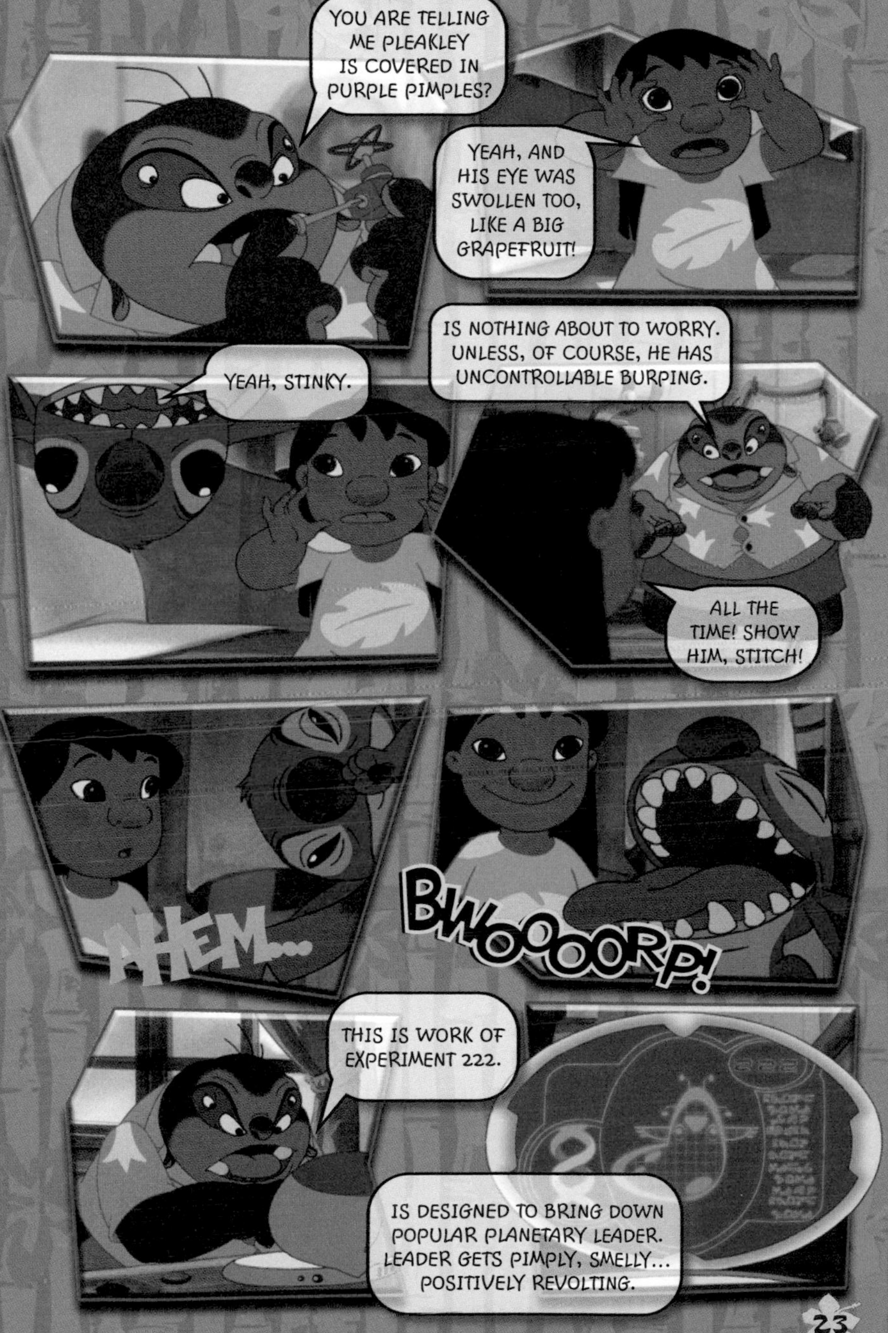
YOU ARE TELLING ME PLEAKLEY IS COVERED IN PURPLE PIMPLES?
YEAH, AND HIS EYE WAS SWOLLEN TOO, LIKE A BIG GRAPEFRUIT!
YEAH, STINKY.
IS NOTHING ABOUT TO WORRY. UNLESS, OF COURSE, HE HAS UNCONTROLLABLE BURPING.
ALL THE TIME! SHOW HIM, STITCH!
AHEM...
BWOOOOORP!
THIS IS WORK OF EXPERIMENT 222.
IS DESIGNED TO BRING DOWN POPULAR PLANETARY LEADER. LEADER GETS PIMPLY, SMELLY... POSITIVELY REVOLTING.

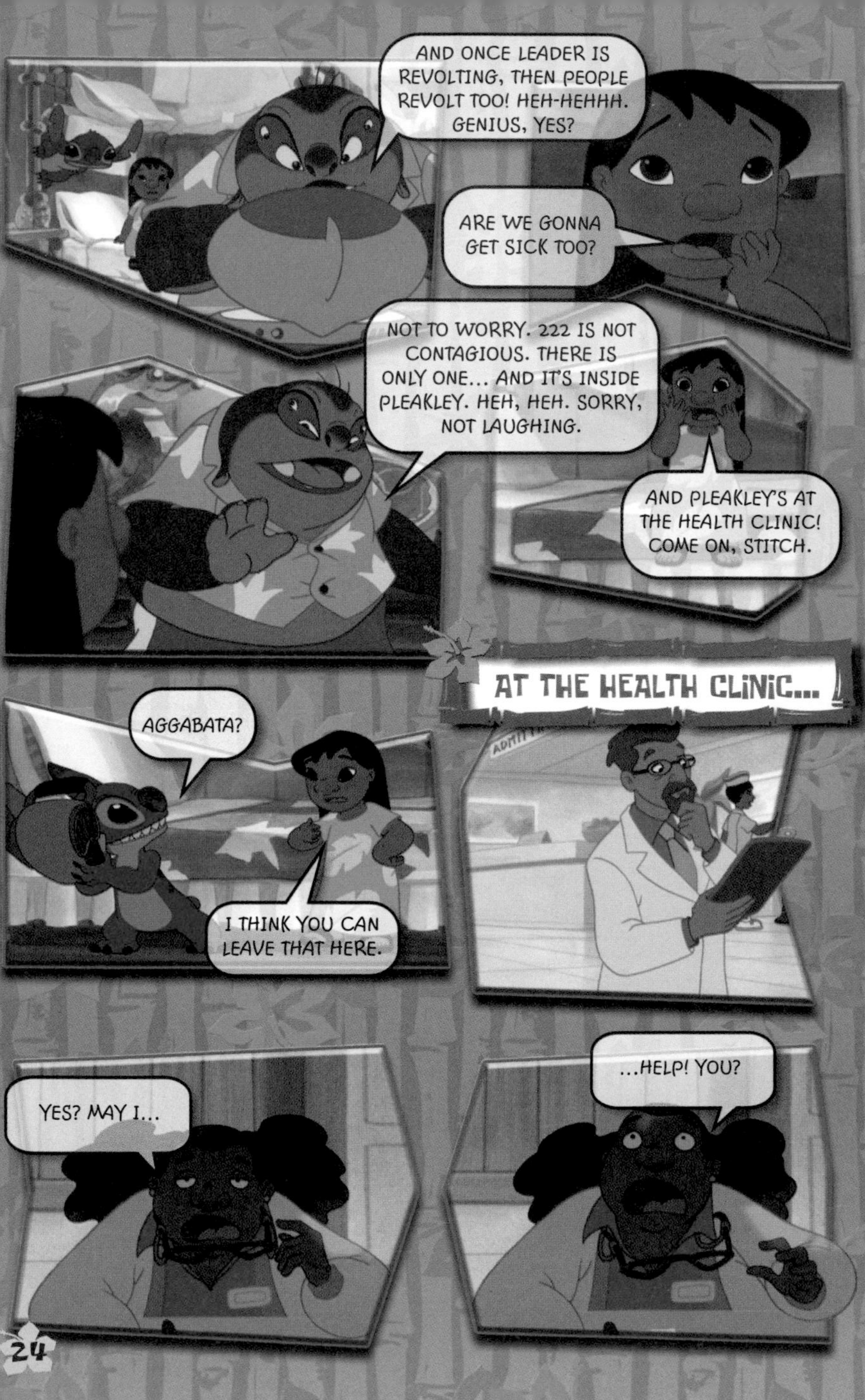
AND ONCE LEADER IS REVOLTING, THEN PEOPLE REVOLT TOO! HEH-HEHHH. GENIUS, YES?
ARE WE GONNA GET SICK TOO?
NOT TO WORRY. 222 IS NOT CONTAGIOUS. THERE IS ONLY ONE... AND IT'S INSIDE PLEAKLEY. HEH, HEH. SORRY, NOT LAUGHING.
AND PLEAKLEY'S AT THE HEALTH CLINIC! COME ON, STITCH.
AT THE HEALTH CLINIC...
AGGABATA?
I THINK YOU CAN LEAVE THAT HERE.
YES? MAY I...
...HELP! YOU?

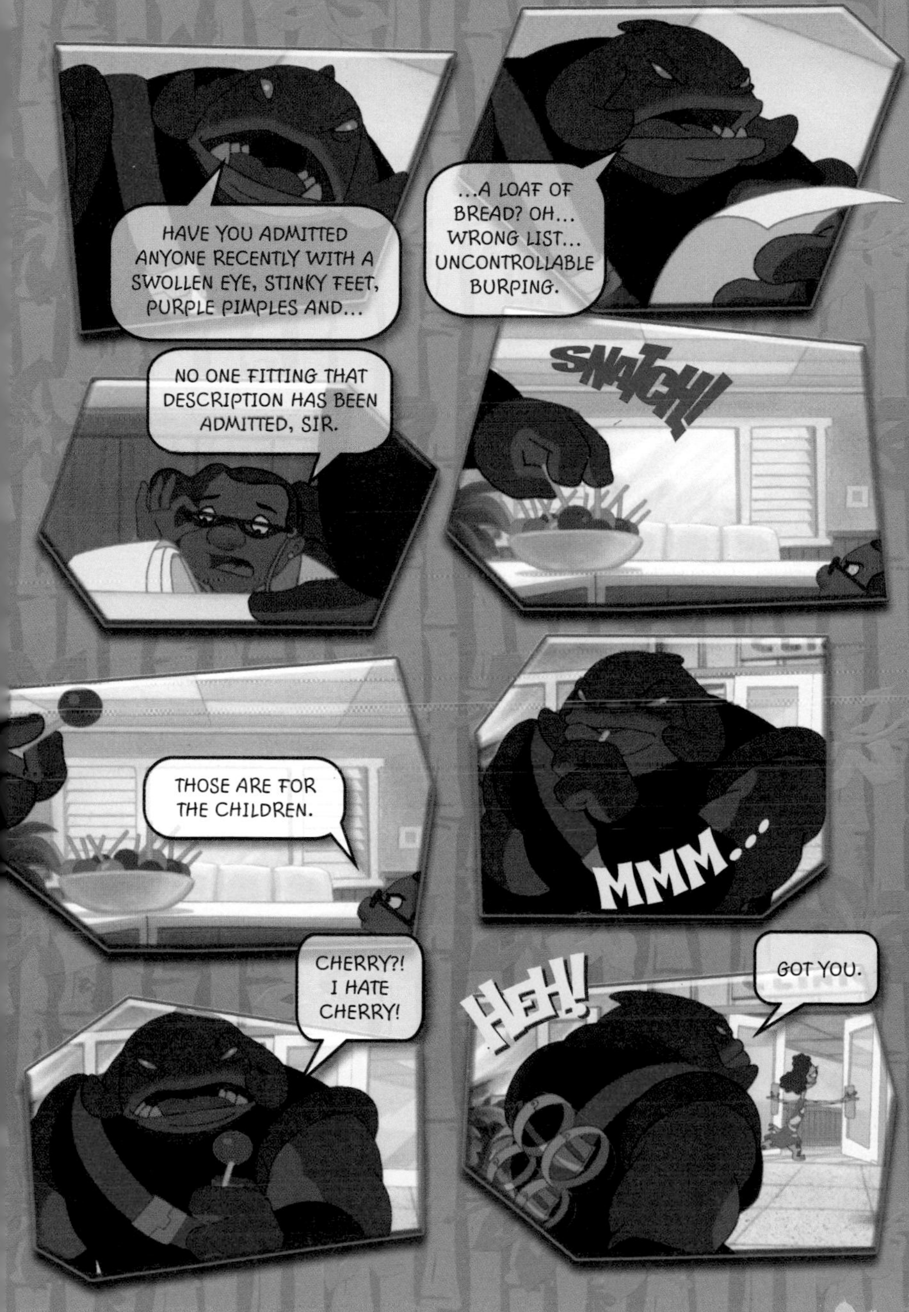
HAVE YOU ADMITTED ANYONE RECENTLY WITH A SWOLLEN EYE, STINKY FEET, PURPLE PIMPLES AND...
...A LOAF OF BREAD? OH... WRONG LIST... UNCONTROLLABLE BURPING.
NO ONE FITTING THAT DESCRIPTION HAS BEEN ADMITTED, SIR.
SNATCH!
THOSE ARE FOR THE CHILDREN.
MMM...
CHERRY?! I HATE CHERRY!
HEH!
GOT YOU.

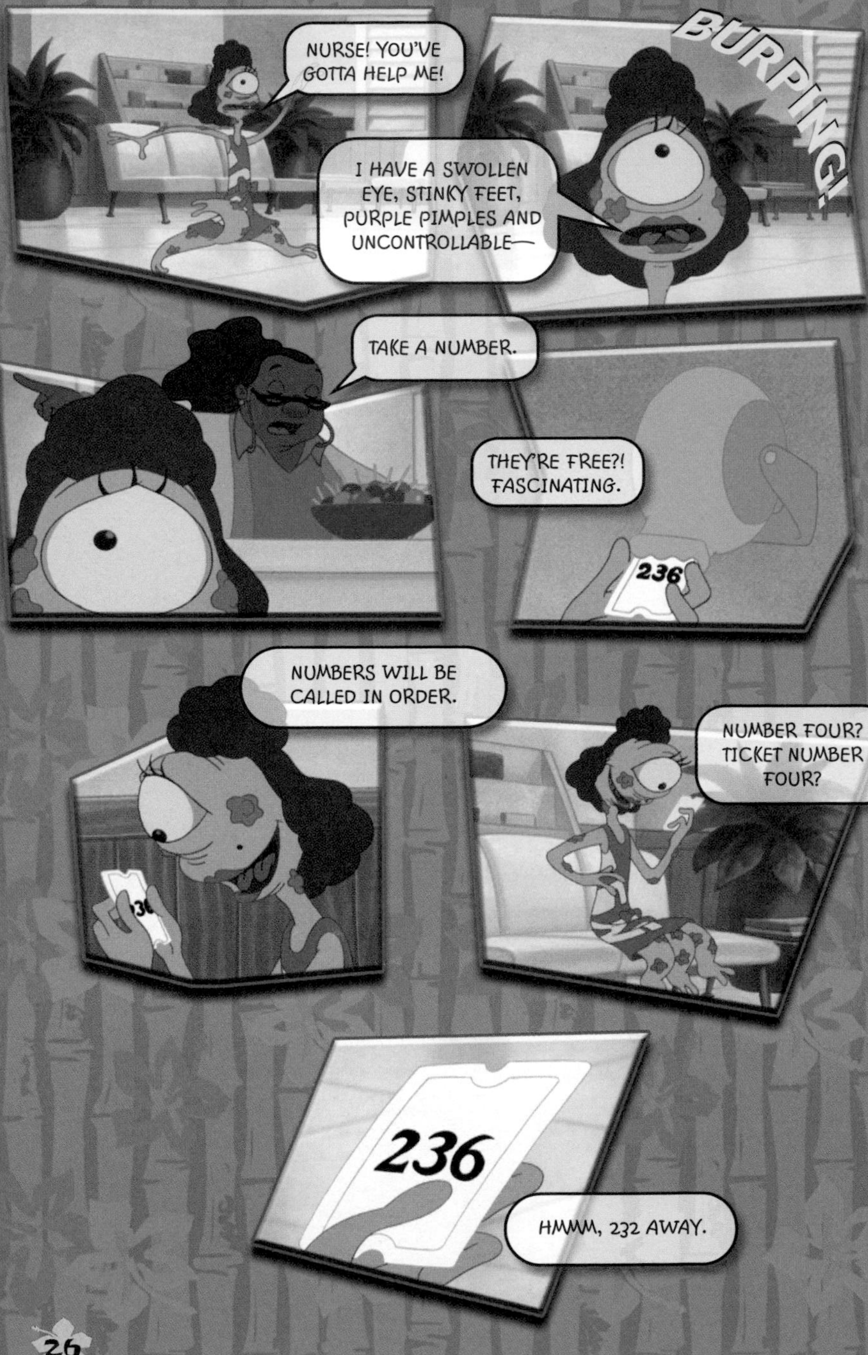
NURSE! YOU'VE GOTTA HELP ME!
BURPING!
I HAVE A SWOLLEN EYE, STINKY FEET, PURPLE PIMPLES AND UNCONTROLLABLE—
TAKE A NUMBER.
THEY'RE FREE?! FASCINATING.
236
NUMBERS WILL BE CALLED IN ORDER.
NUMBER FOUR? TICKET NUMBER FOUR?
236
HMMM, 232 AWAY.

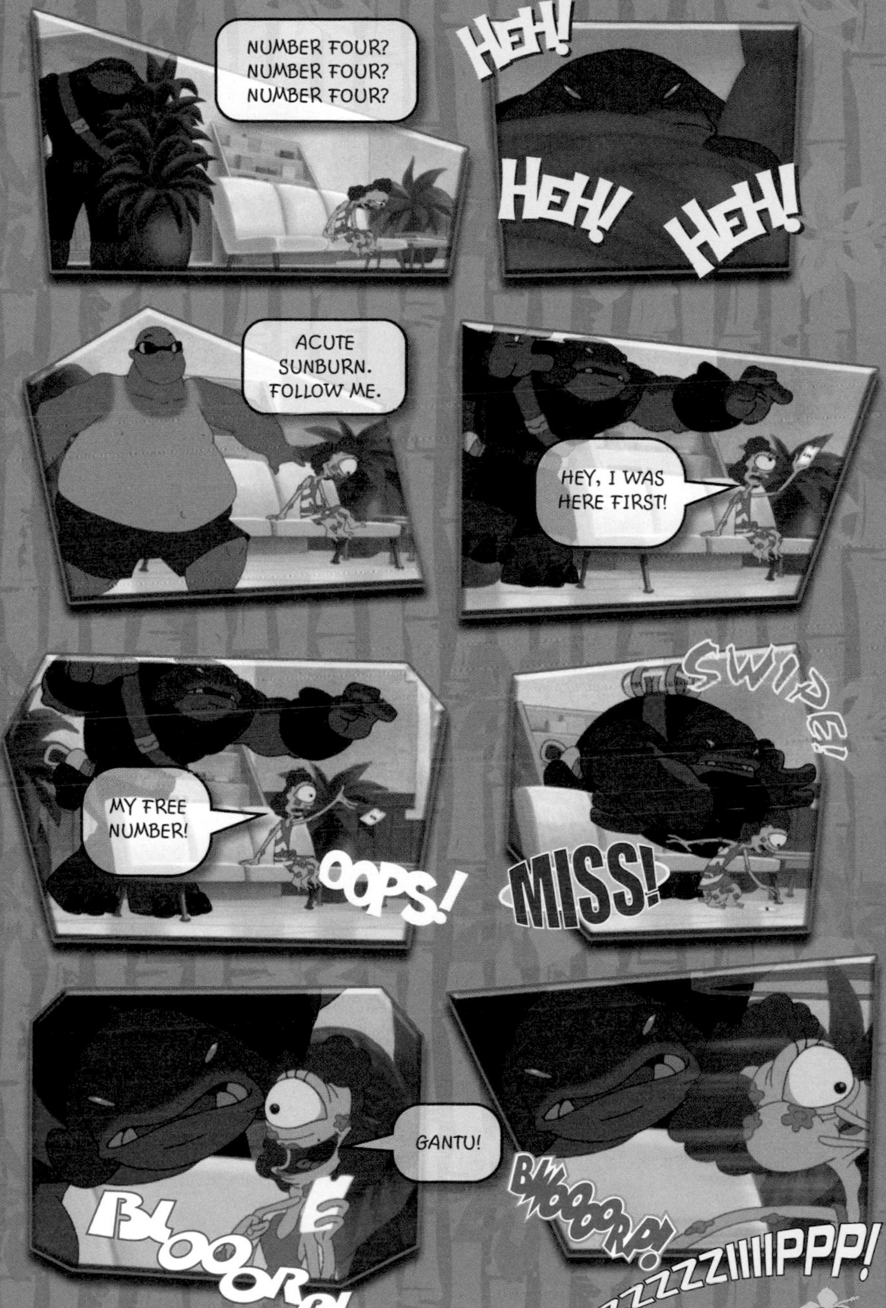

NUMBER FOUR? NUMBER FOUR? NUMBER FOUR?
HEH!
HEH!
HEH!
ACUTE SUNBURN. FOLLOW ME.
HEY, I WAS HERE FIRST!
MY FREE NUMBER!
OOPS!
SWIPE!
MISS!
GANTU!
BLOOORP!
BWOOOORP!
ZZZZZIIIIPPP!

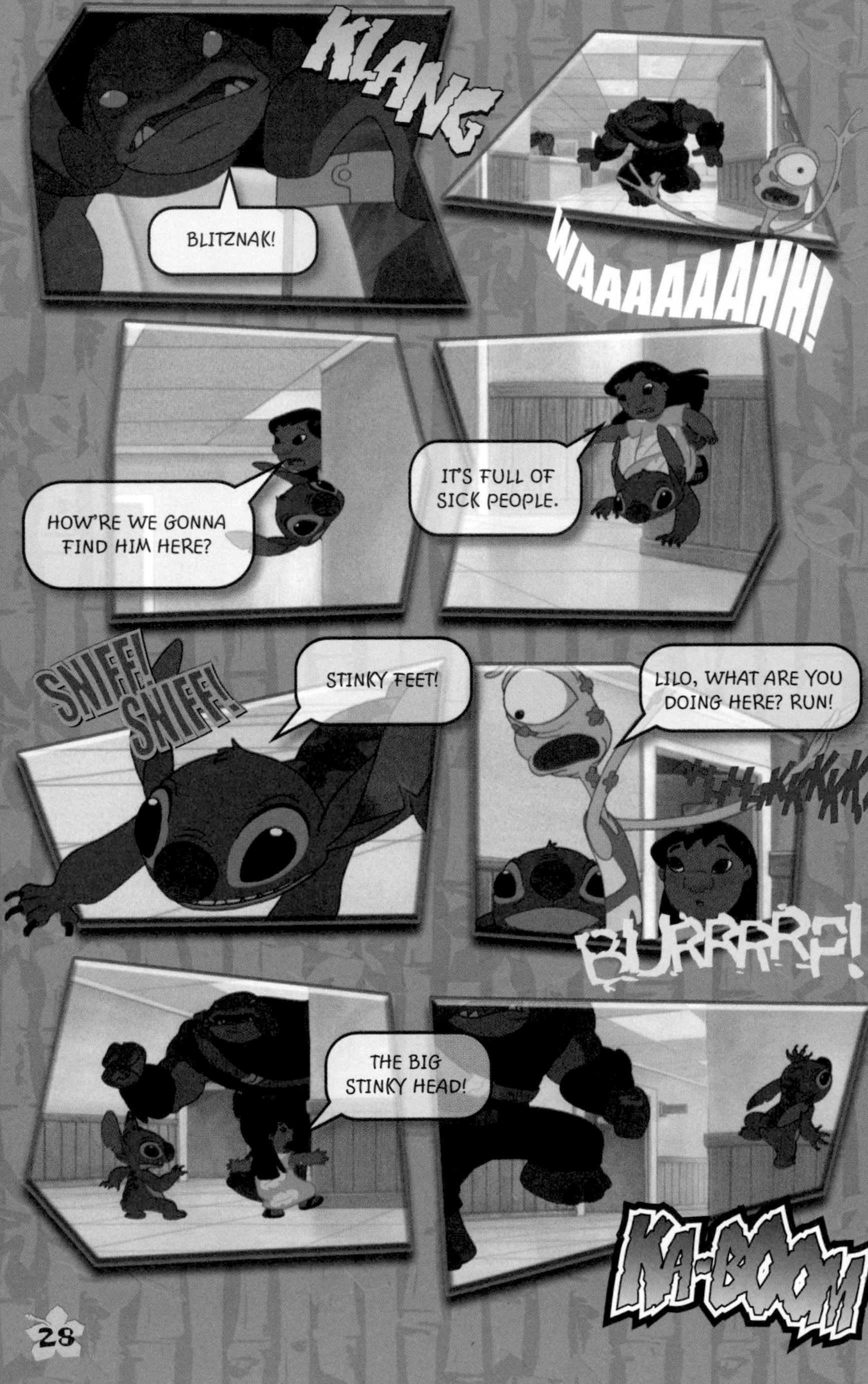

KLANG
BLITZNAK!
WAAAAAAHH!
HOW'RE WE GONNA FIND HIM HERE?
IT'S FULL OF SICK PEOPLE.
SNIFF! SNIFF!
STINKY FEET!
LILO, WHAT ARE YOU DOING HERE? RUN!
BURRRRP!
THE BIG STINKY HEAD!
KA-BOOM

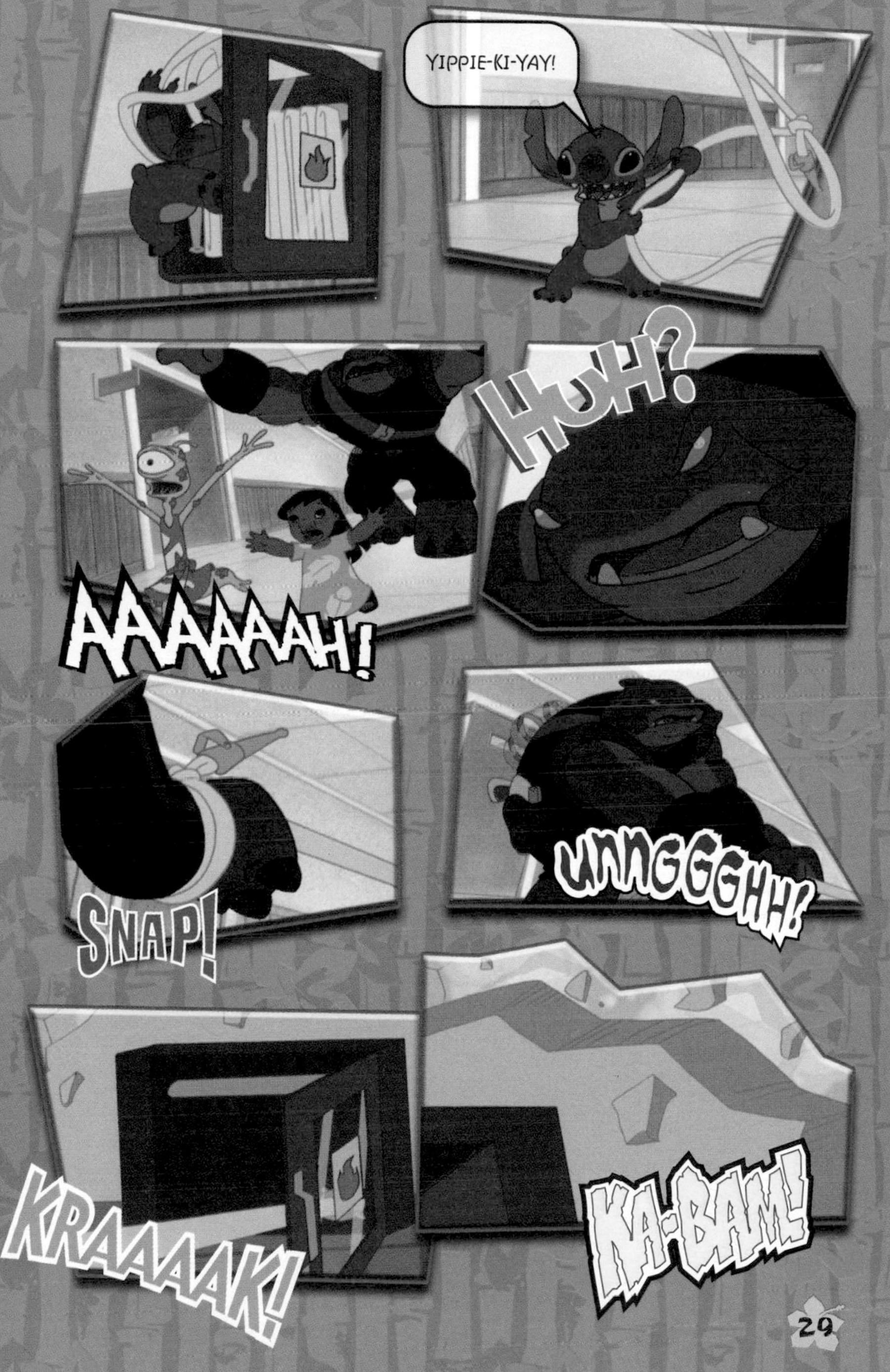
YIPPIE-KI-YAY!
AAAAAAAH!
HUH?
SNAP!
UNNGGGHH!
KRAAAAK!
KA-BAM!

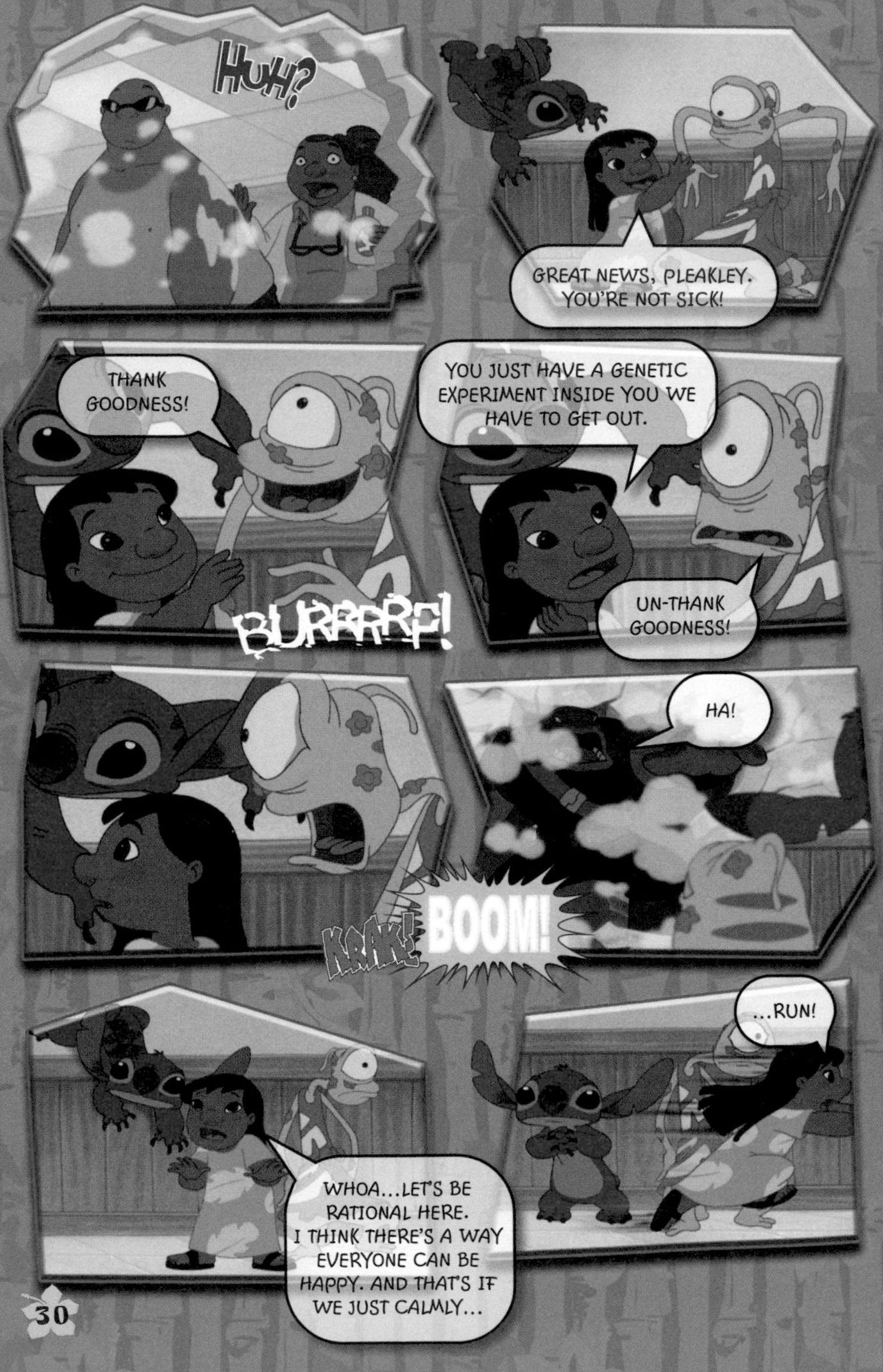

HUH?
GREAT NEWS, PLEAKLEY. YOU'RE NOT SICK!
THANK GOODNESS!
YOU JUST HAVE A GENETIC EXPERIMENT INSIDE YOU WE HAVE TO GET OUT.
BURRRRP!
UN-THANK GOODNESS!
HA!
KRAK!
BOOM!
WHOA...LET'S BE RATIONAL HERE. I THINK THERE'S A WAY EVERYONE CAN BE HAPPY. AND THAT'S IF WE JUST CALMLY...
...RUN!

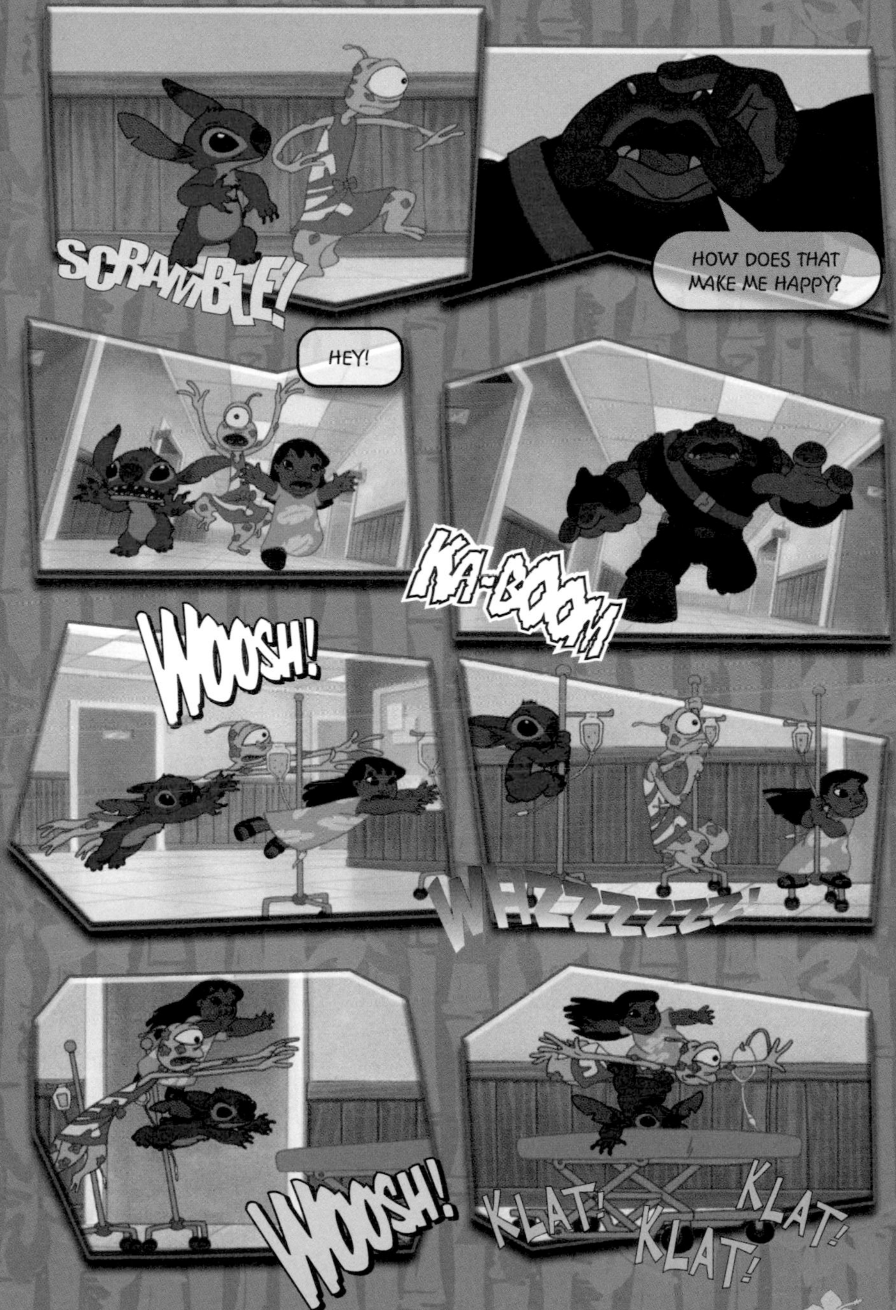
SCRAMBLE!
HOW DOES THAT MAKE ME HAPPY?
HEY!
KA-BOOM
WOOSH!
WHZZZZZZZ!
WOOSH!
KLAT!
KLAT!
KLAT!

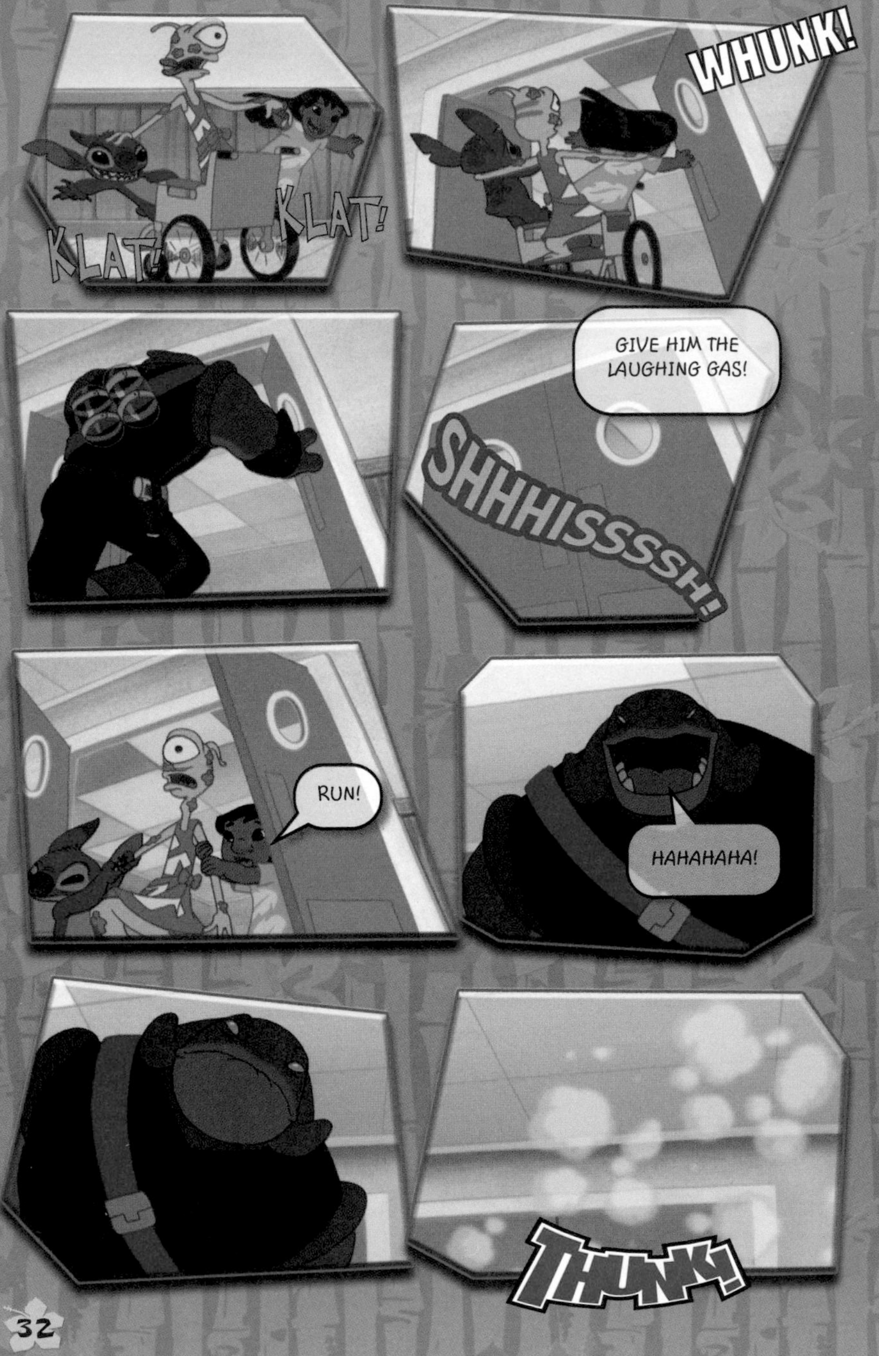
KLAT!
KLAT!
WHUNK!
GIVE HIM THE LAUGHING GAS!
SHHHISSSSSH!
RUN!
HAHAHAHA!
THUNK!

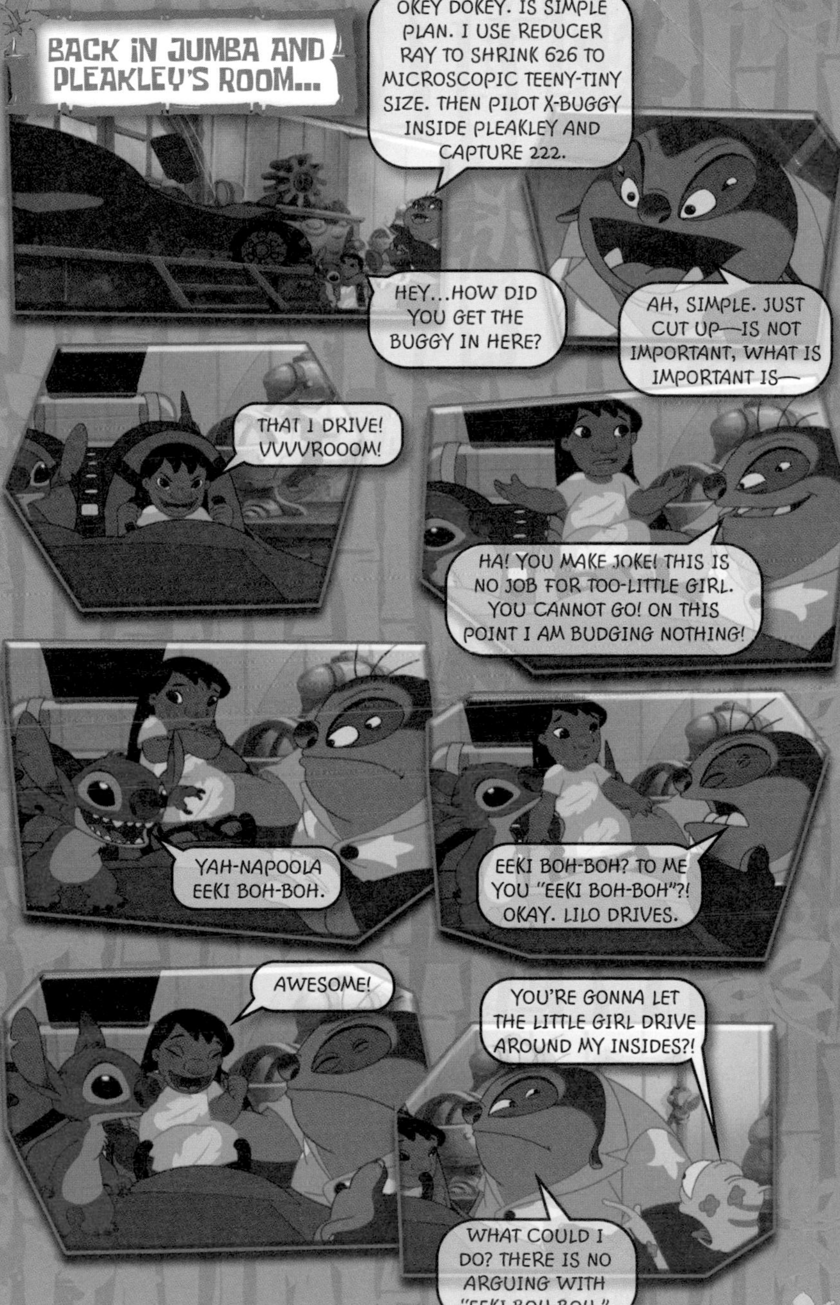
BACK IN JUMBA AND PLEAKLEY'S ROOM...
OKEY DOKEY. IS SIMPLE PLAN. I USE REDUCER RAY TO SHRINK 626 TO MICROSCOPIC TEENY-TINY SIZE. THEN PILOT X-BUGGY INSIDE PLEAKLEY AND CAPTURE 222.
HEY...HOW DID YOU GET THE BUGGY IN HERE?
AH, SIMPLE. JUST CUT UP—IS NOT IMPORTANT, WHAT IS IMPORTANT IS—
THAT I DRIVE! VVVVROOOM!
HA! YOU MAKE JOKE! THIS IS NO JOB FOR TOO-LITTLE GIRL. YOU CANNOT GO! ON THIS POINT I AM BUDGING NOTHING!
YAH-NAPOOLA EEKI BOH-BOH.
EEKI BOH-BOH? TO ME YOU "EEKI BOH-BOH"?! OKAY. LILO DRIVES.
AWESOME!
YOU'RE GONNA LET THE LITTLE GIRL DRIVE AROUND MY INSIDES?!
WHAT COULD I DO? THERE IS NO ARGUING WITH "EEKI BOH-BOH."

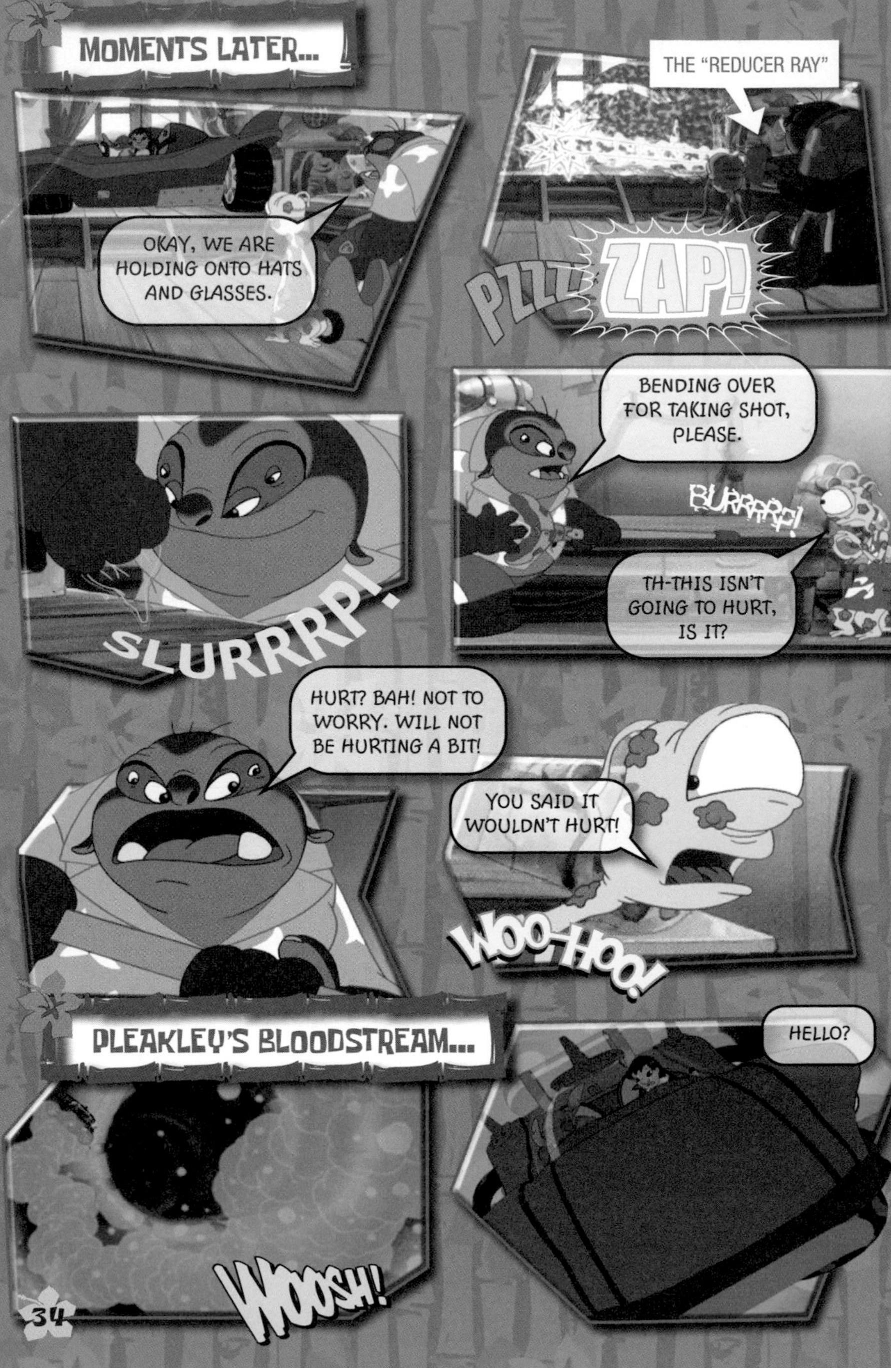
MOMENTS LATER...
OKAY, WE ARE HOLDING ONTO HATS AND GLASSES.
THE "REDUCER RAY"
PZZZ
ZAP!
SLURRRP!
BENDING OVER FOR TAKING SHOT, PLEASE.
BURRRRP!
TH-THIS ISN'T GOING TO HURT, IS IT?
HURT? BAH! NOT TO WORRY. WILL NOT BE HURTING A BIT!
YOU SAID IT WOULDN'T HURT!
WOO-HOO!
PLEAKLEY'S BLOODSTREAM...
WOOSH!
HELLO?

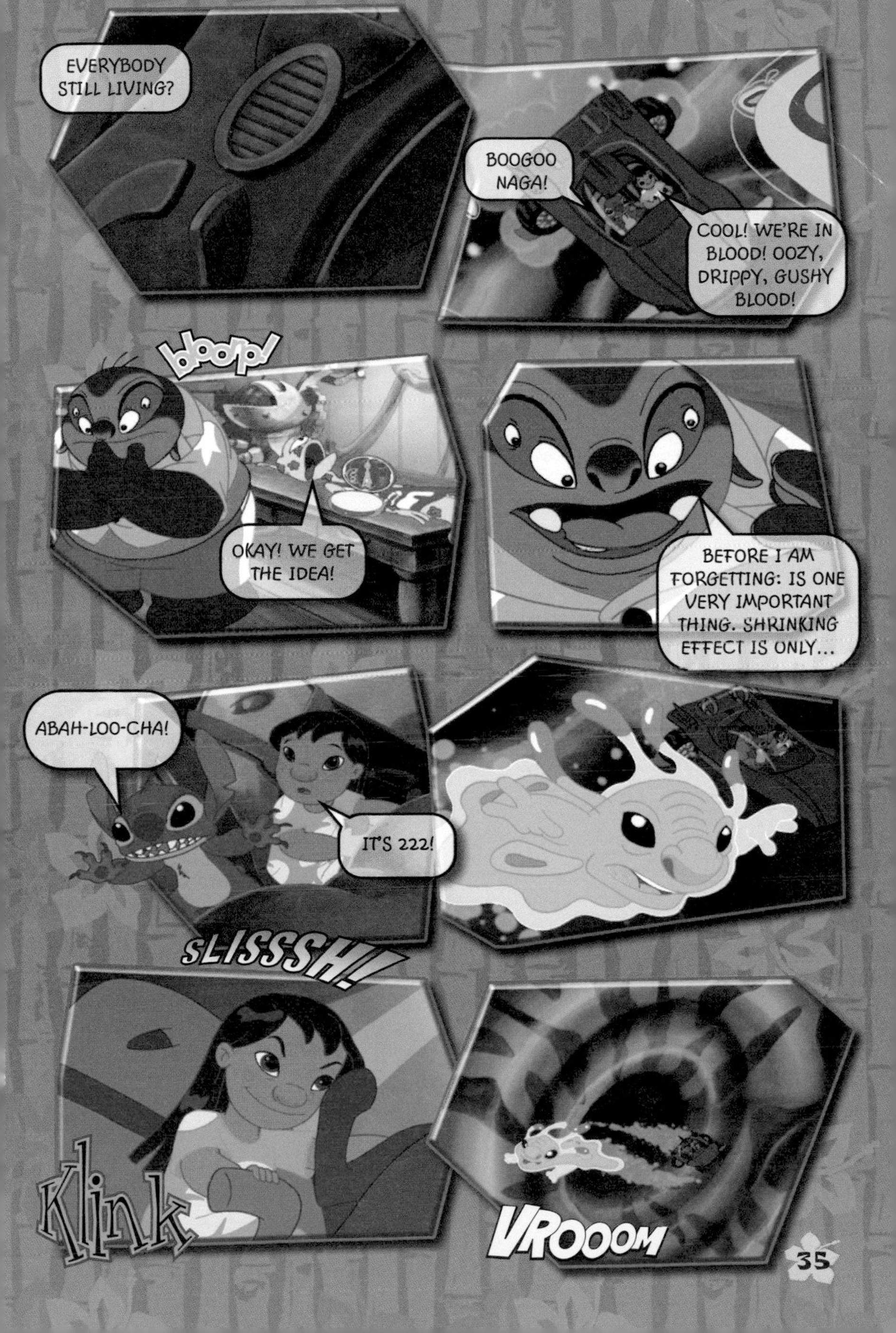
EVERYBODY STILL LIVING?
BOOGOO NAGA!
COOL! WE'RE IN BLOOD! OOZY, DRIPPY, GUSHY BLOOD!
bloop!
OKAY! WE GET THE IDEA!
BEFORE I AM FORGETTING: IS ONE VERY IMPORTANT THING. SHRINKING EFFECT IS ONLY...
ABAH-LOO-CHA!
IT'S 222!
SLISSSH!!
Klink
VROOOM

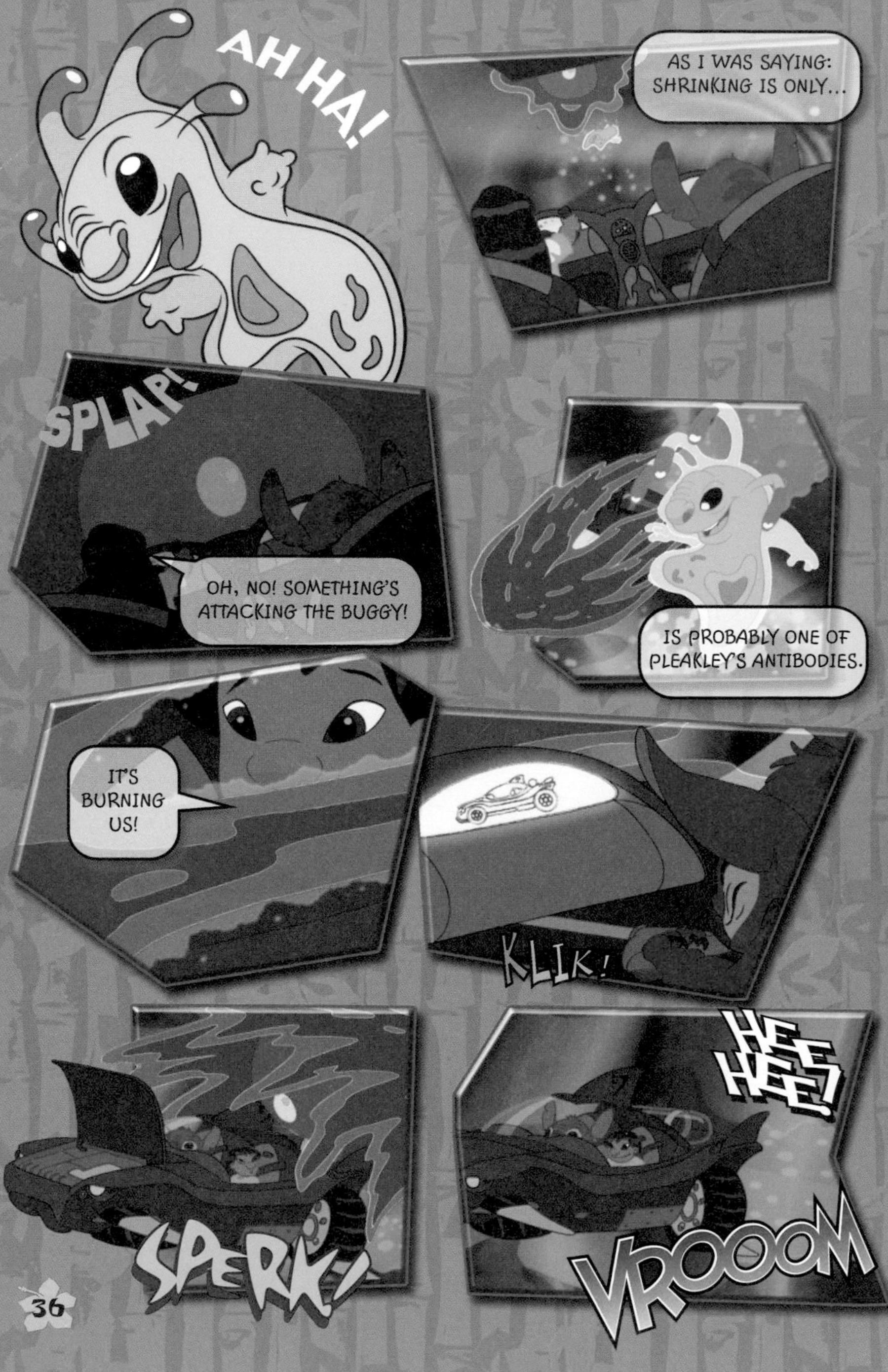
AH HA!
AS I WAS SAYING: SHRINKING IS ONLY...
SPLAP!
OH, NO! SOMETHING'S ATTACKING THE BUGGY!
IS PROBABLY ONE OF PLEAKLEY'S ANTIBODIES.
IT'S BURNING US!
KLIK!
SPERK!
HEE HEE!
VROOOM

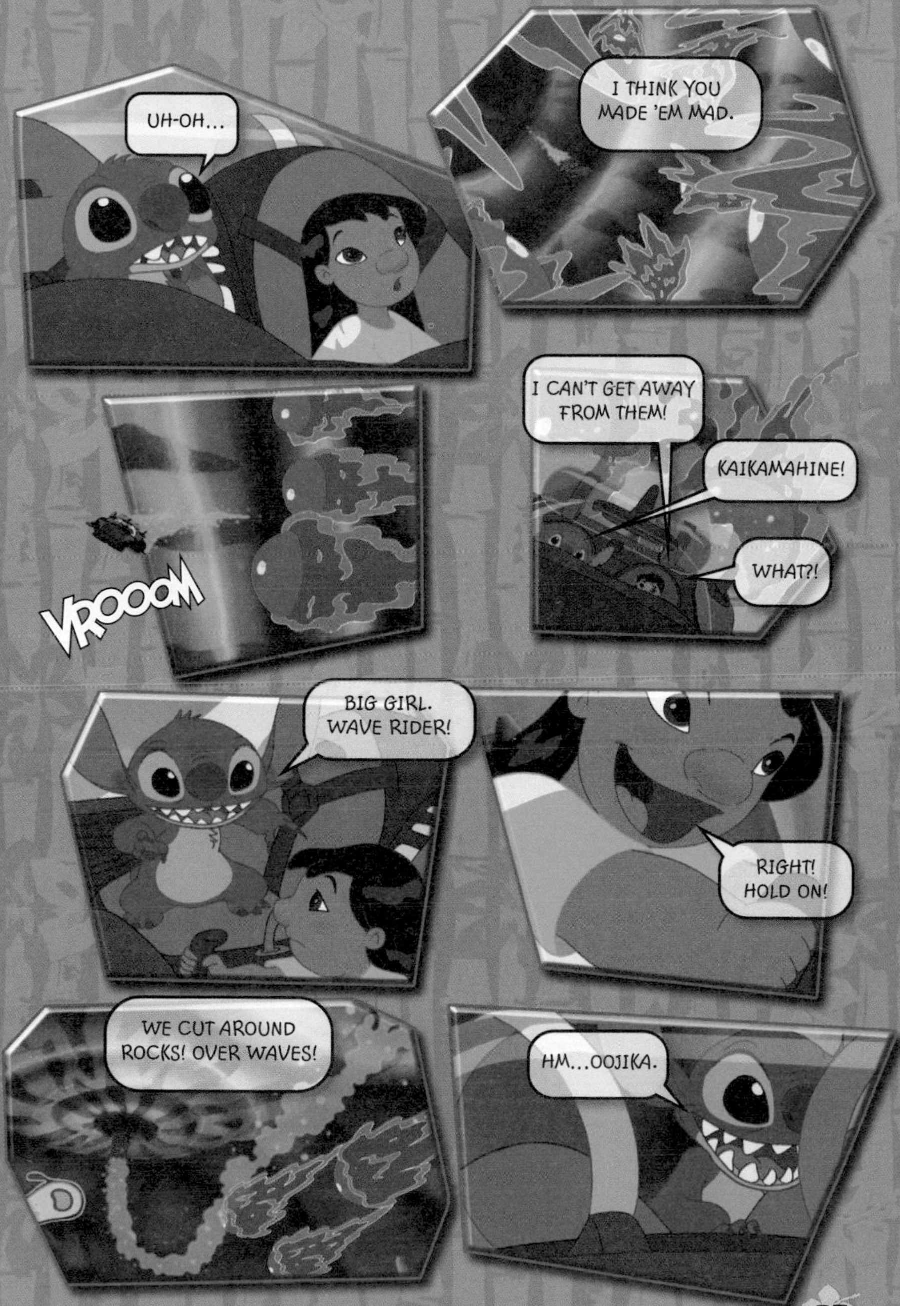
UH-OH...
I THINK YOU MADE 'EM MAD.
VROOOM
I CAN'T GET AWAY FROM THEM!
KAIKAMAHINE!
WHAT?!
BIG GIRL. WAVE RIDER!
RIGHT! HOLD ON!
WE CUT AROUND ROCKS! OVER WAVES!
HM...OOJIKA.

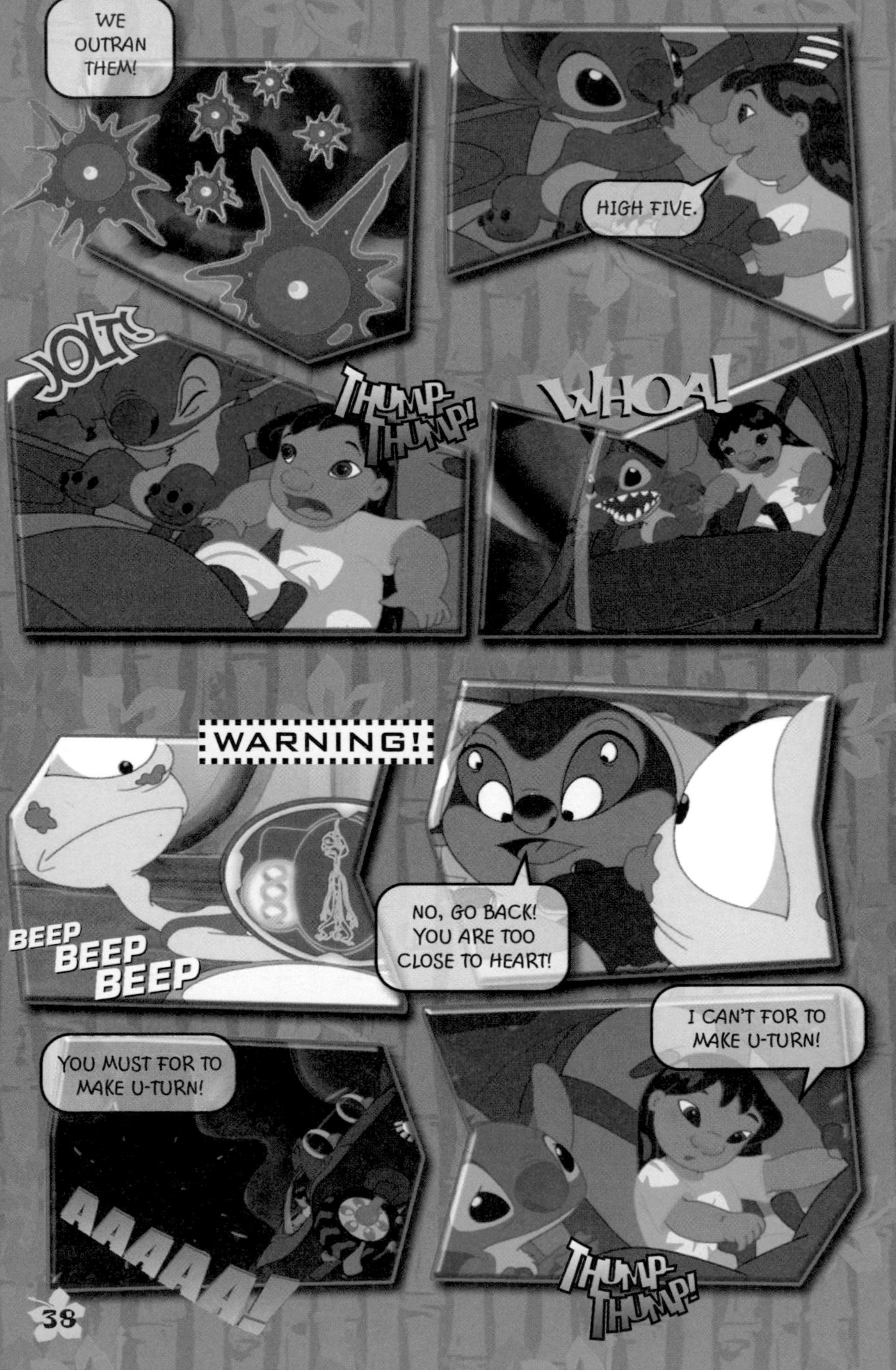
WE OUTRAN THEM!
HIGH FIVE.
JOLT!
THUMP-THUMP!
WHOA!
WARNING!
BEEP BEEP BEEP
NO, GO BACK! YOU ARE TOO CLOSE TO HEART!
YOU MUST FOR TO MAKE U-TURN!
AAAAAA!
I CAN'T FOR TO MAKE U-TURN!
THUMP-THUMP!

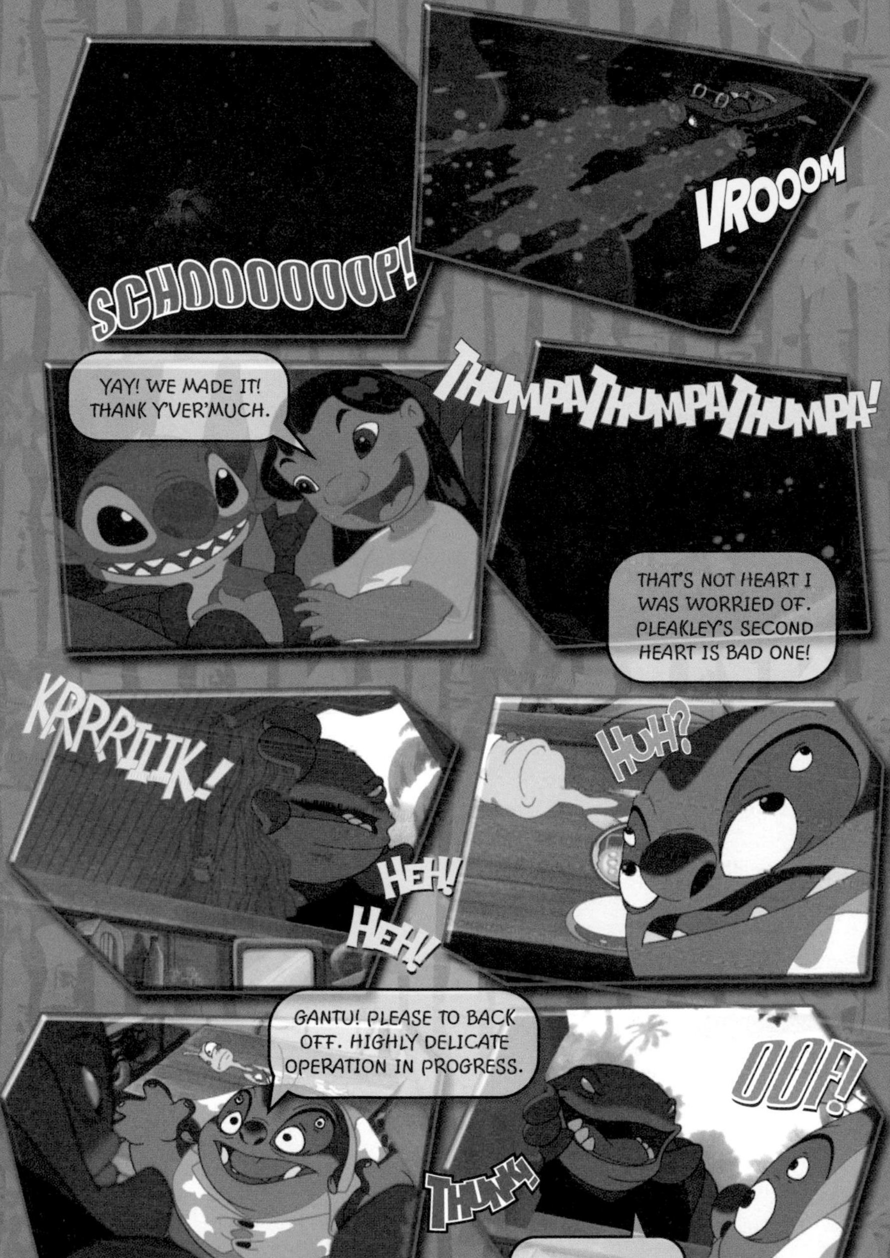

SCHOOOOOOOP!
VROOOM
YAY! WE MADE IT! THANK Y'VER'MUCH.
THUMPATHUMPATHUMPA!
THAT'S NOT HEART I WAS WORRIED OF. PLEAKLEY'S SECOND HEART IS BAD ONE!
KRRRIIIK!
HEH! HEH!
HUH?
GANTU! PLEASE TO BACK OFF. HIGHLY DELICATE OPERATION IN PROGRESS.
OOF!
THUNK!
IDIOT SCIENTIST.

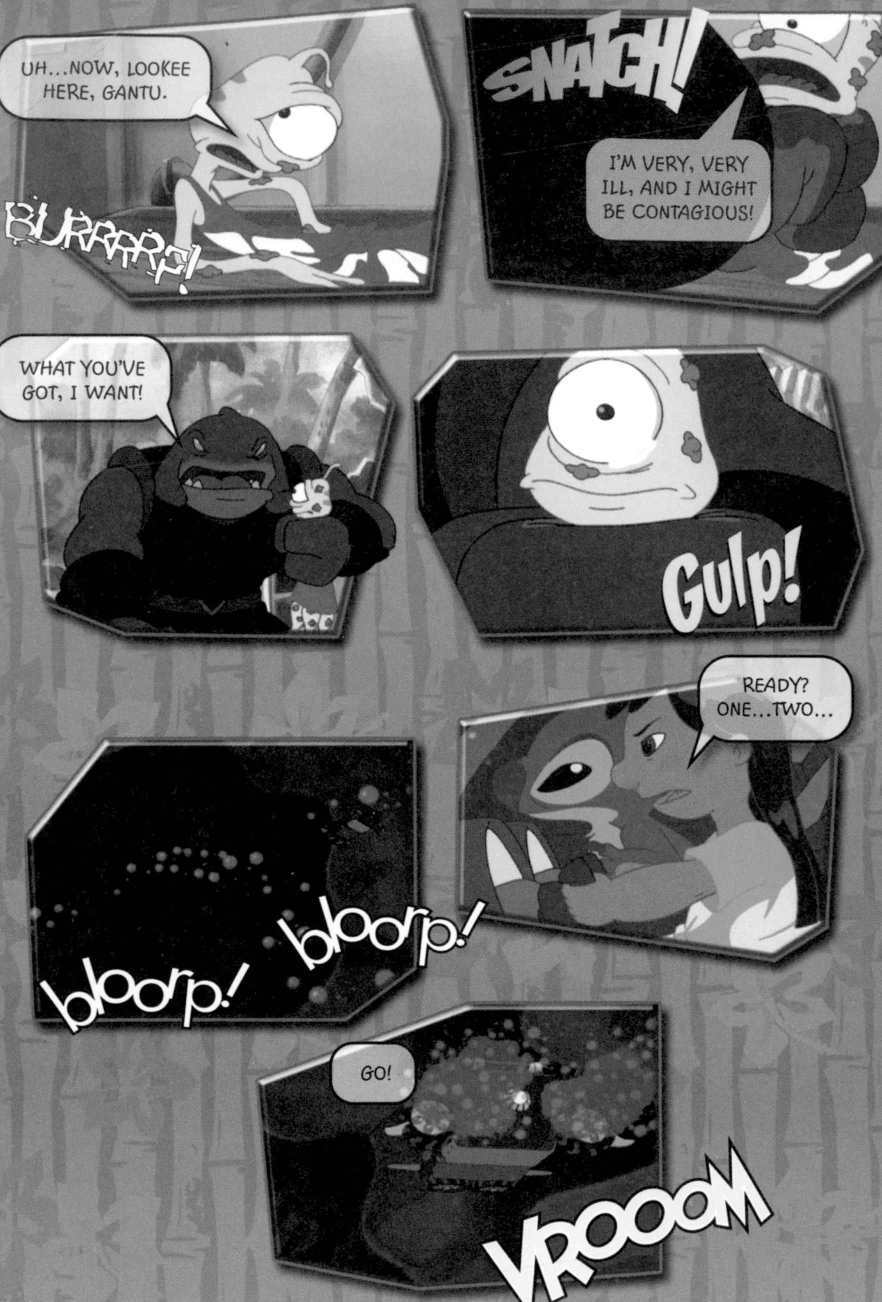
UH...NOW, LOOKEE HERE, GANTU.
BURRRRP!
SNATCH!
I'M VERY, VERY ILL, AND I MIGHT BE CONTAGIOUS!
WHAT YOU'VE GOT, I WANT!
Gulp!
READY? ONE...TWO...
bloorp! bloorp!
GO!
VROOOM

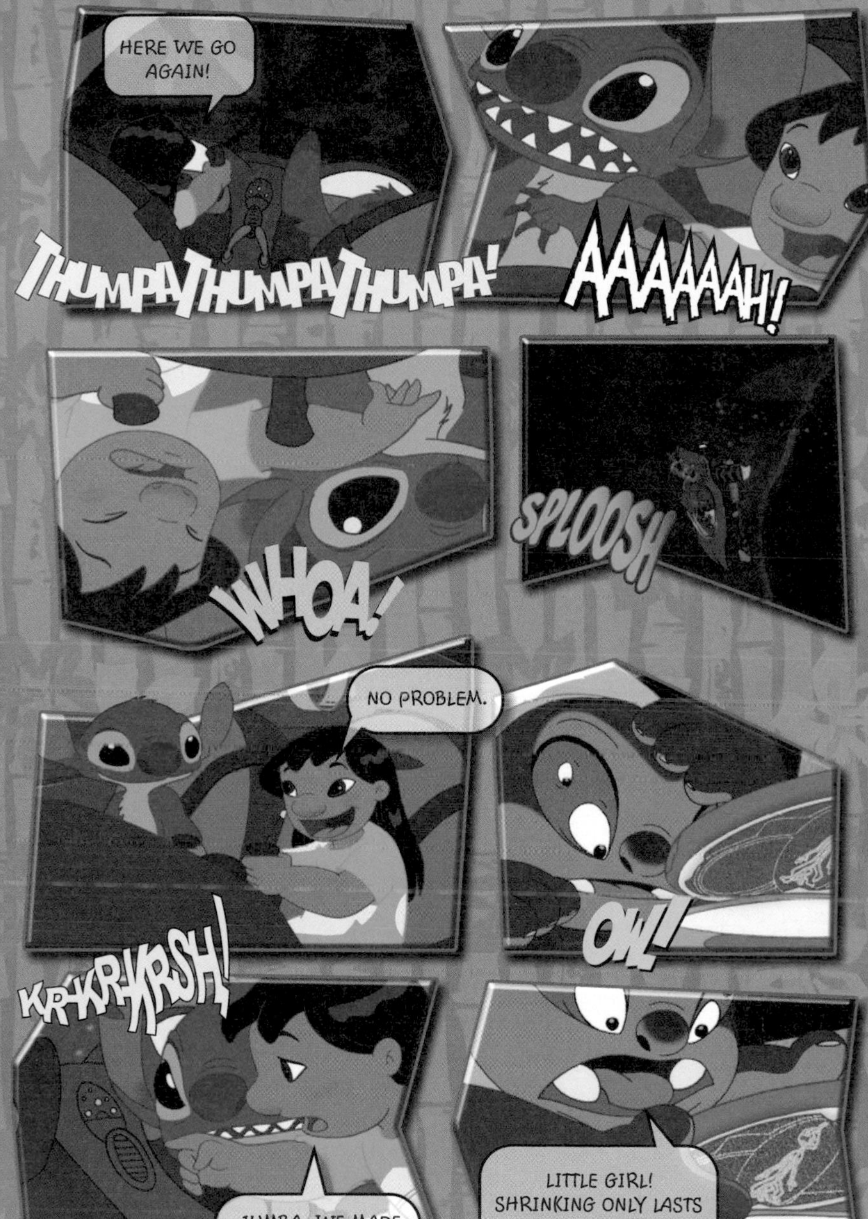
HERE WE GO AGAIN!
THUMPATHUMPATHUMPA!
AAAAAAH!
WHOA!
SPLOOSH
NO PROBLEM.
OW!
KRKRKRSH!
JUMBA, WE MADE IT...JUMBA?
LITTLE GIRL! SHRINKING ONLY LASTS FOR ONE HOUR!

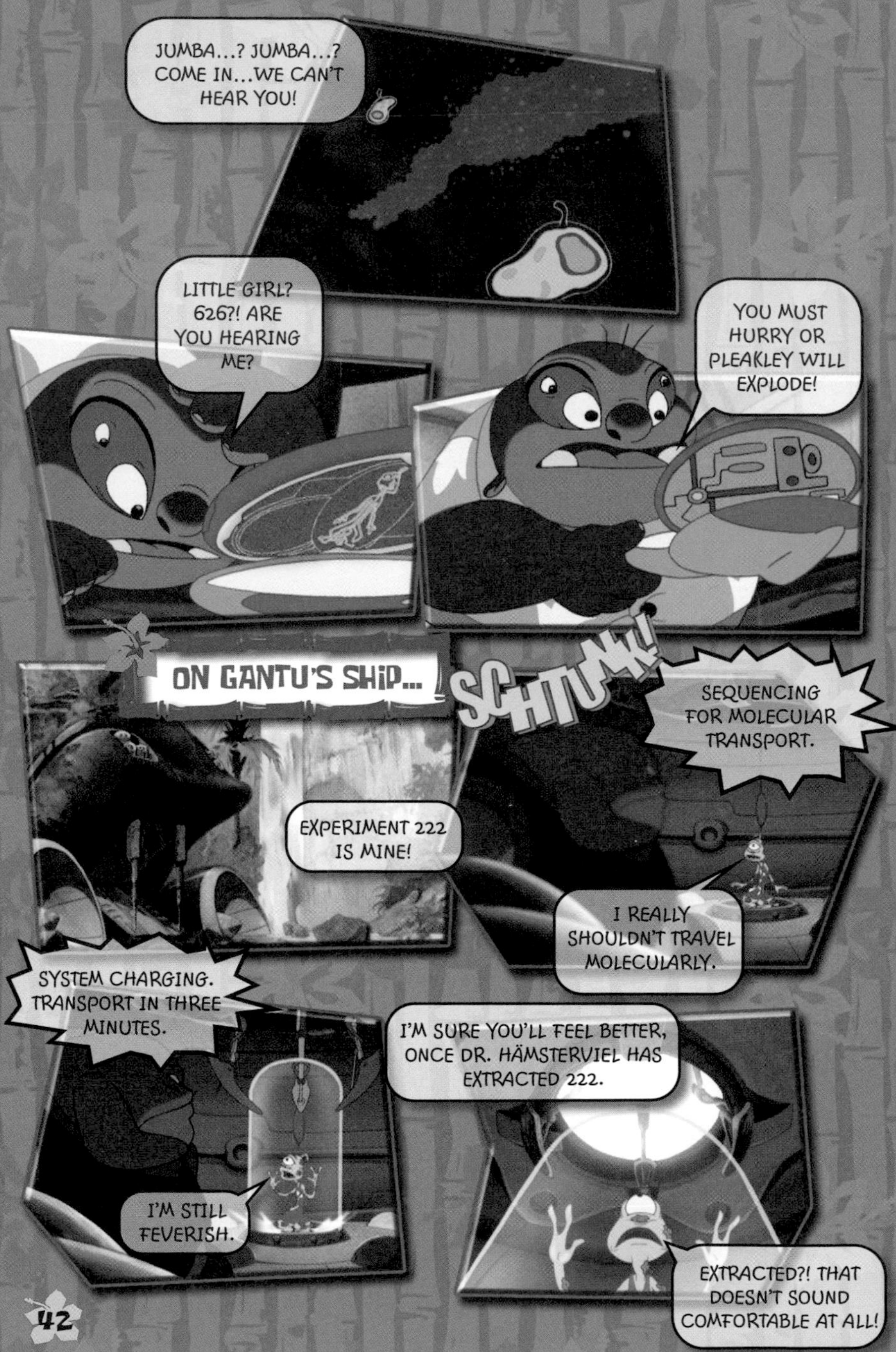
JUMBA...? JUMBA...? COME IN...WE CAN'T HEAR YOU!
LITTLE GIRL? 626?! ARE YOU HEARING ME?
YOU MUST HURRY OR PLEAKLEY WILL EXPLODE!
ON GANTU'S SHIP...
SCHTUNK!
SEQUENCING FOR MOLECULAR TRANSPORT.
EXPERIMENT 222 IS MINE!
I REALLY SHOULDN'T TRAVEL MOLECULARLY.
SYSTEM CHARGING. TRANSPORT IN THREE MINUTES.
I'M STILL FEVERISH.
I'M SURE YOU'LL FEEL BETTER, ONCE DR. HÄMSTERVIEL HAS EXTRACTED 222.
EXTRACTED?! THAT DOESN'T SOUND COMFORTABLE AT ALL!

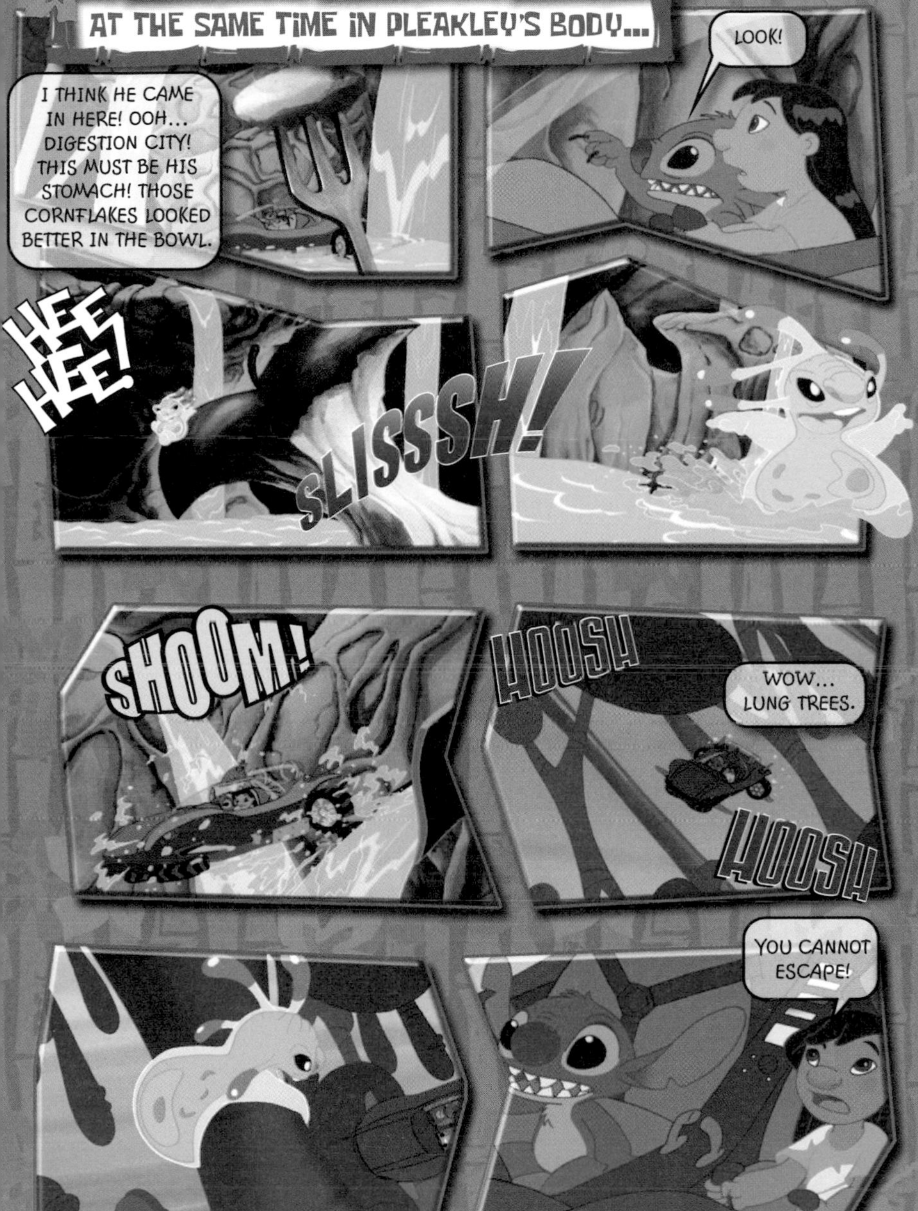
AT THE SAME TIME IN PLEAKLEY'S BODY...
I THINK HE CAME IN HERE! OOH... DIGESTION CITY! THIS MUST BE HIS STOMACH! THOSE CORNFLAKES LOOKED BETTER IN THE BOWL.
LOOK!
HEE HEE!
SLISSSH!
SHOOM!
WHOOSH
WOW... LUNG TREES.
WHOOSH
YOU CANNOT ESCAPE!

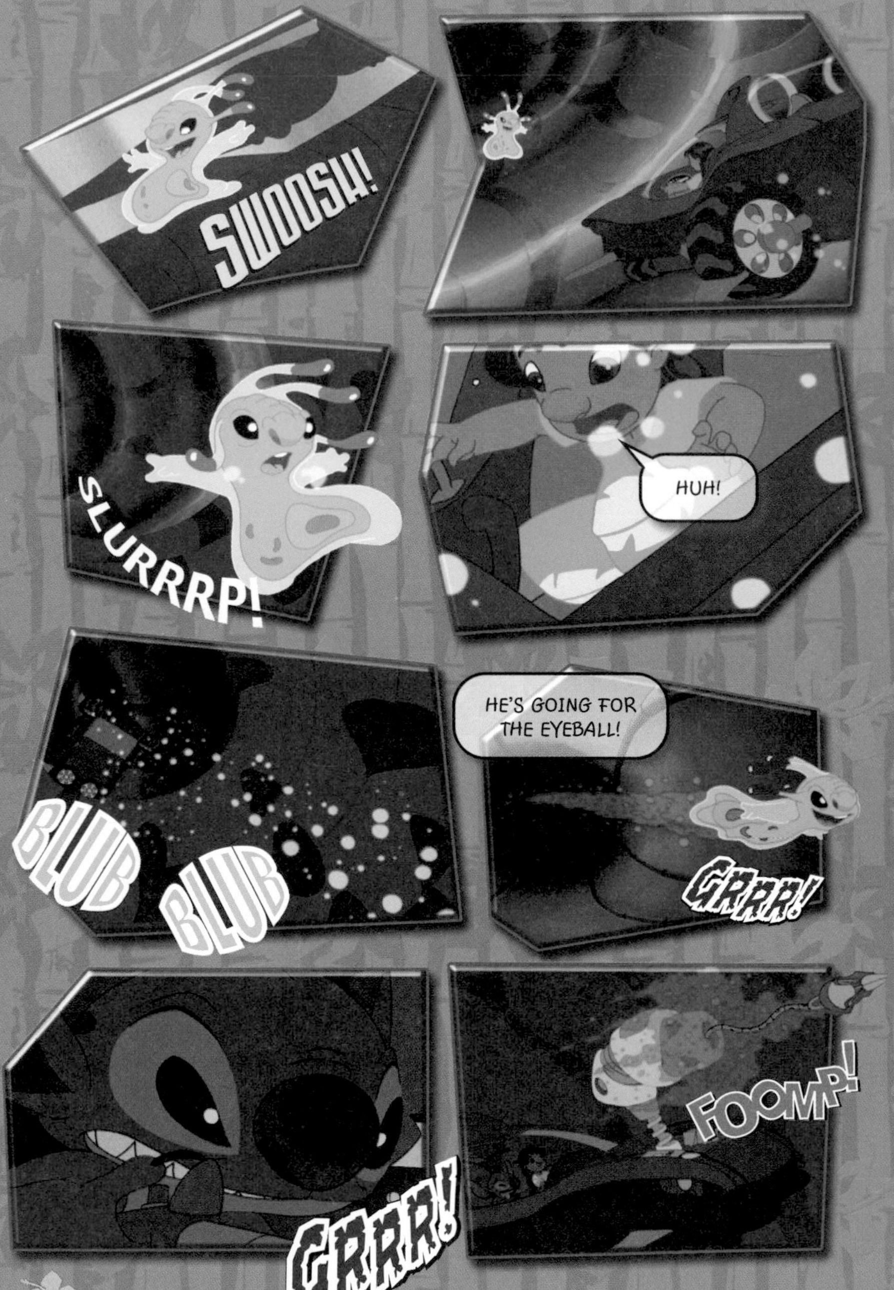
SWOOSH!
SLURRRP!
HUH!
BLUB
BLUB
HE'S GOING FOR THE EYEBALL!
GRRR!
GRRR!
FOOMP!

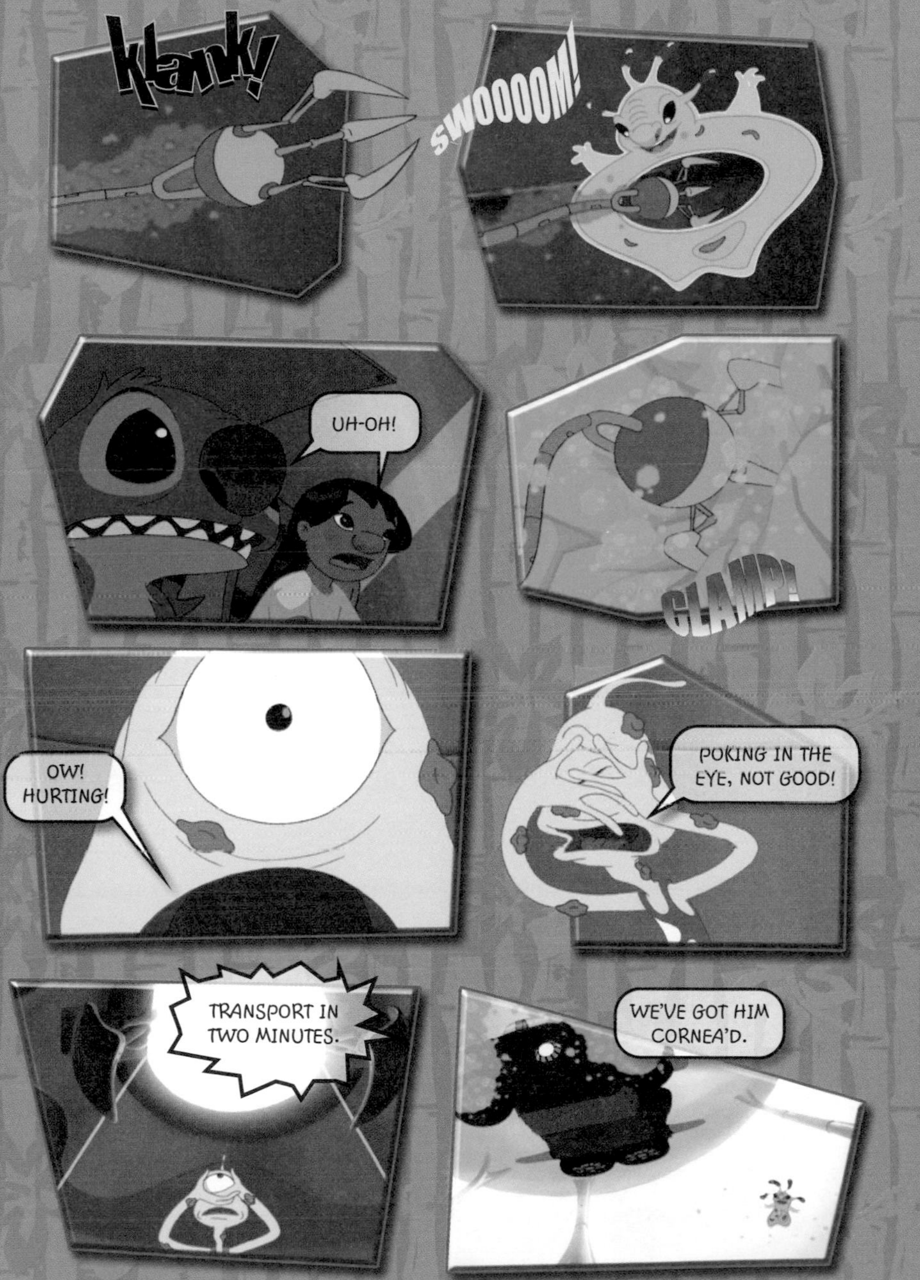
KLANK!
SWOOOOM!
UH-OH!
CLAMP!
OW! HURTING!
POKING IN THE EYE, NOT GOOD!
TRANSPORT IN TWO MINUTES.
WE'VE GOT HIM CORNEA'D.

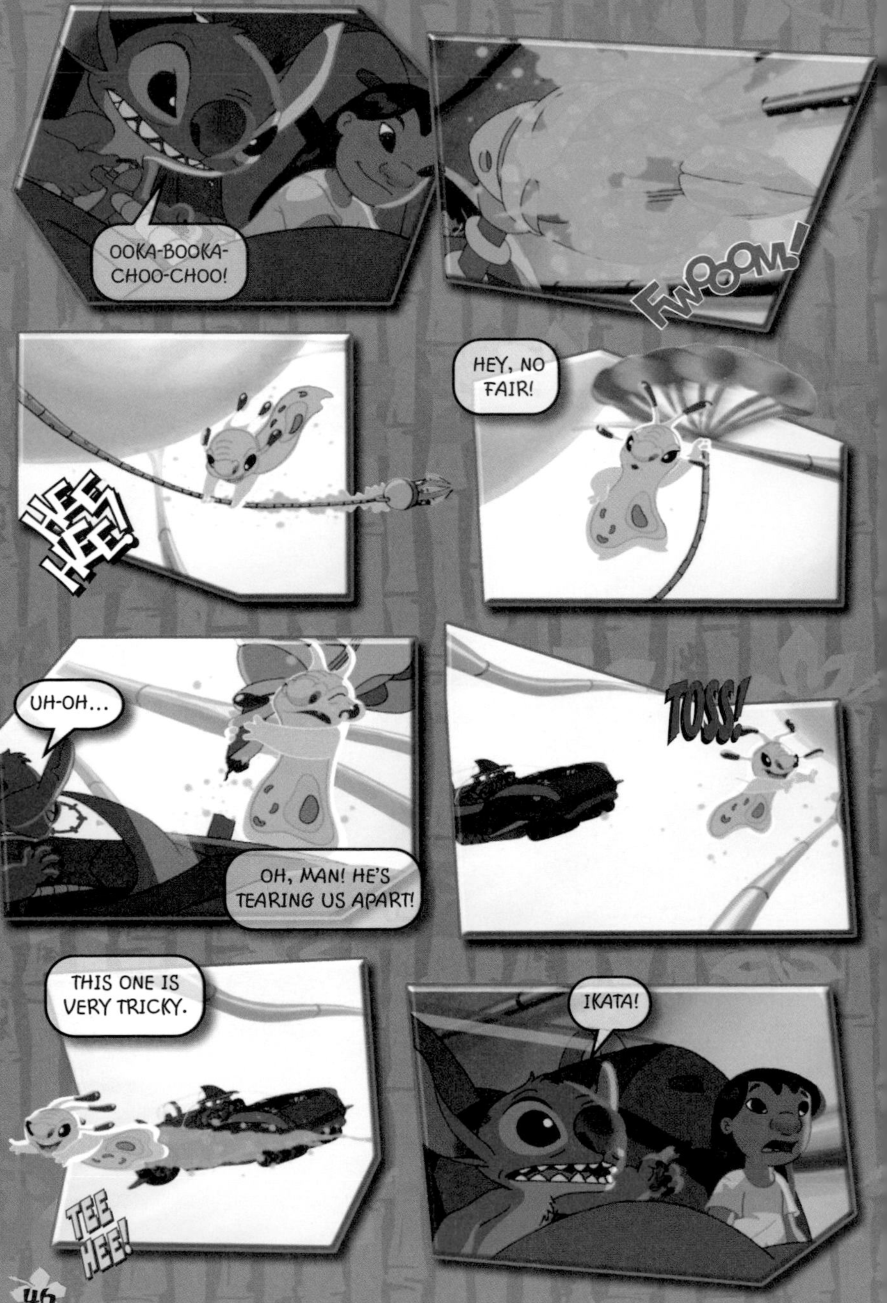
OOKA-BOOKA-CHOO-CHOO!
FWOOM!
HEE HEE!
HEY, NO FAIR!
UH-OH...
OH, MAN! HE'S TEARING US APART!
TOSS!
THIS ONE IS VERY TRICKY.
TEE HEE!
IKATA!

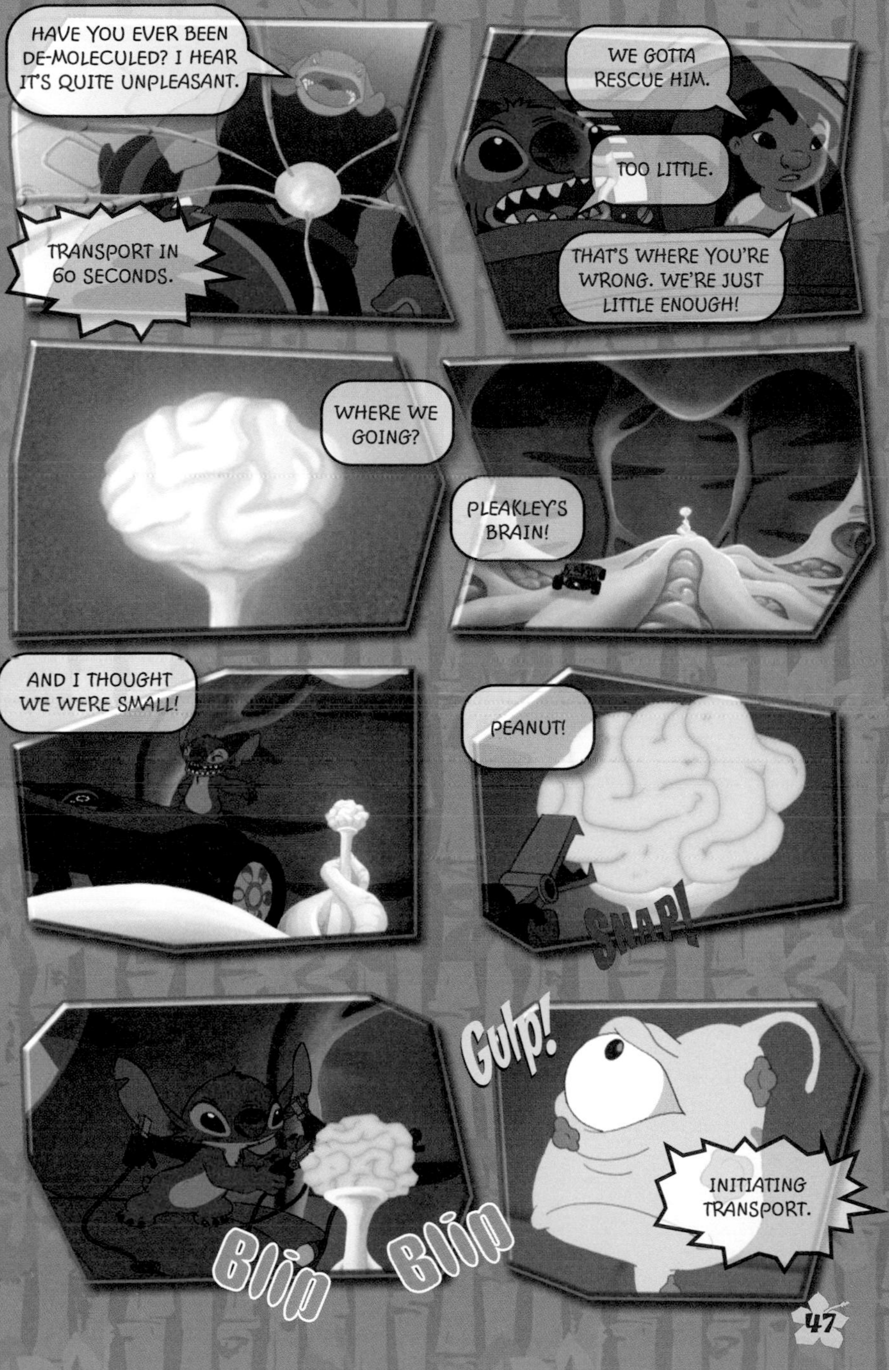

HAVE YOU EVER BEEN DE-MOLECULED? I HEAR IT'S QUITE UNPLEASANT.
TRANSPORT IN 60 SECONDS.
WE GOTTA RESCUE HIM.
TOO LITTLE.
THAT'S WHERE YOU'RE WRONG. WE'RE JUST LITTLE ENOUGH!
WHERE WE GOING?
PLEAKLEY'S BRAIN!
AND I THOUGHT WE WERE SMALL!
PEANUT!
SNAP!
Blip
Blip
Gulp!
INITIATING TRANSPORT.

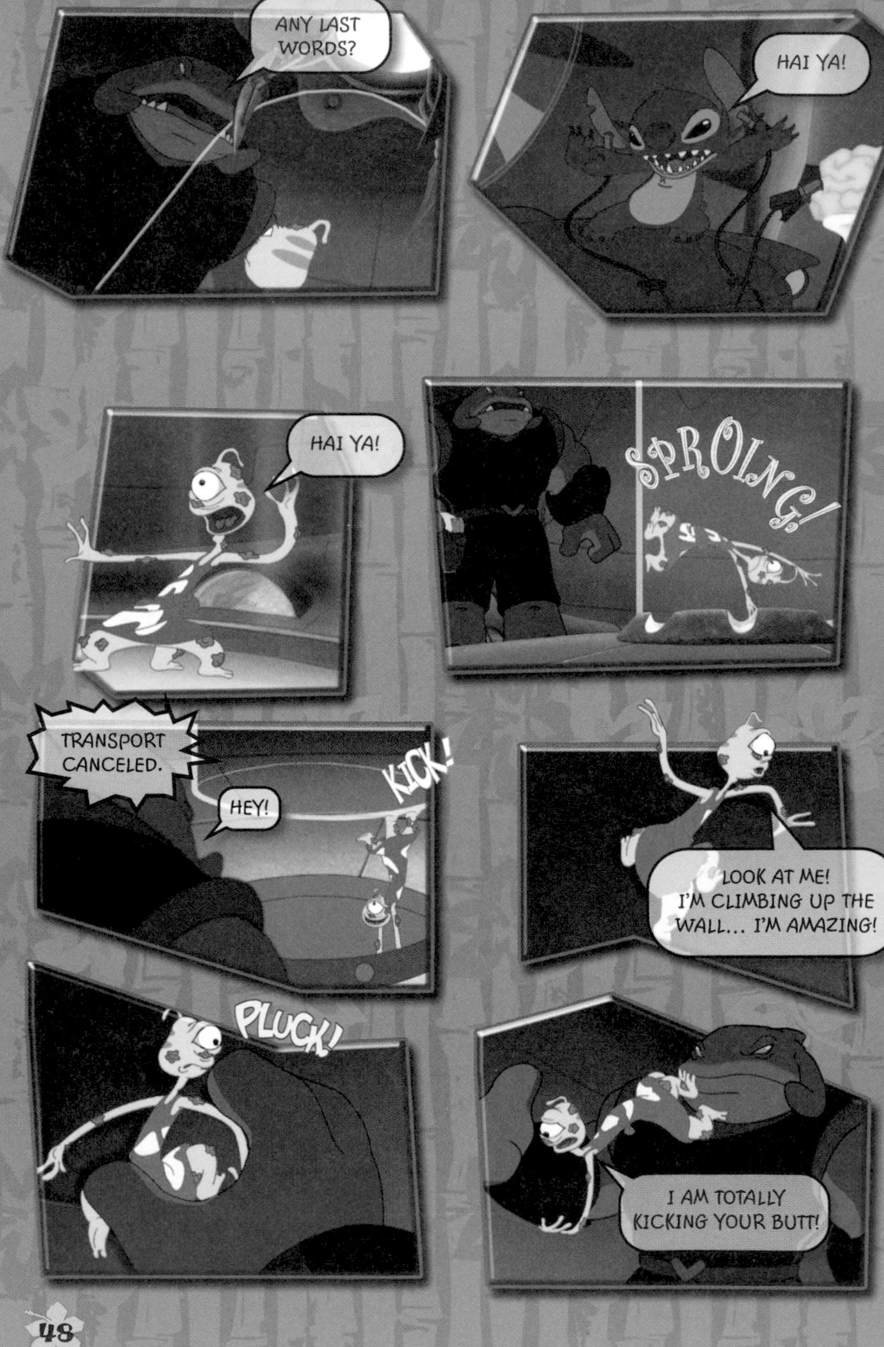
ANY LAST WORDS?
HAI YA!
HAI YA!
SPROING!
TRANSPORT CANCELED.
HEY!
KICK!
LOOK AT ME! I'M CLIMBING UP THE WALL… I'M AMAZING!
PLUCK!
I AM TOTALLY KICKING YOUR BUTT!

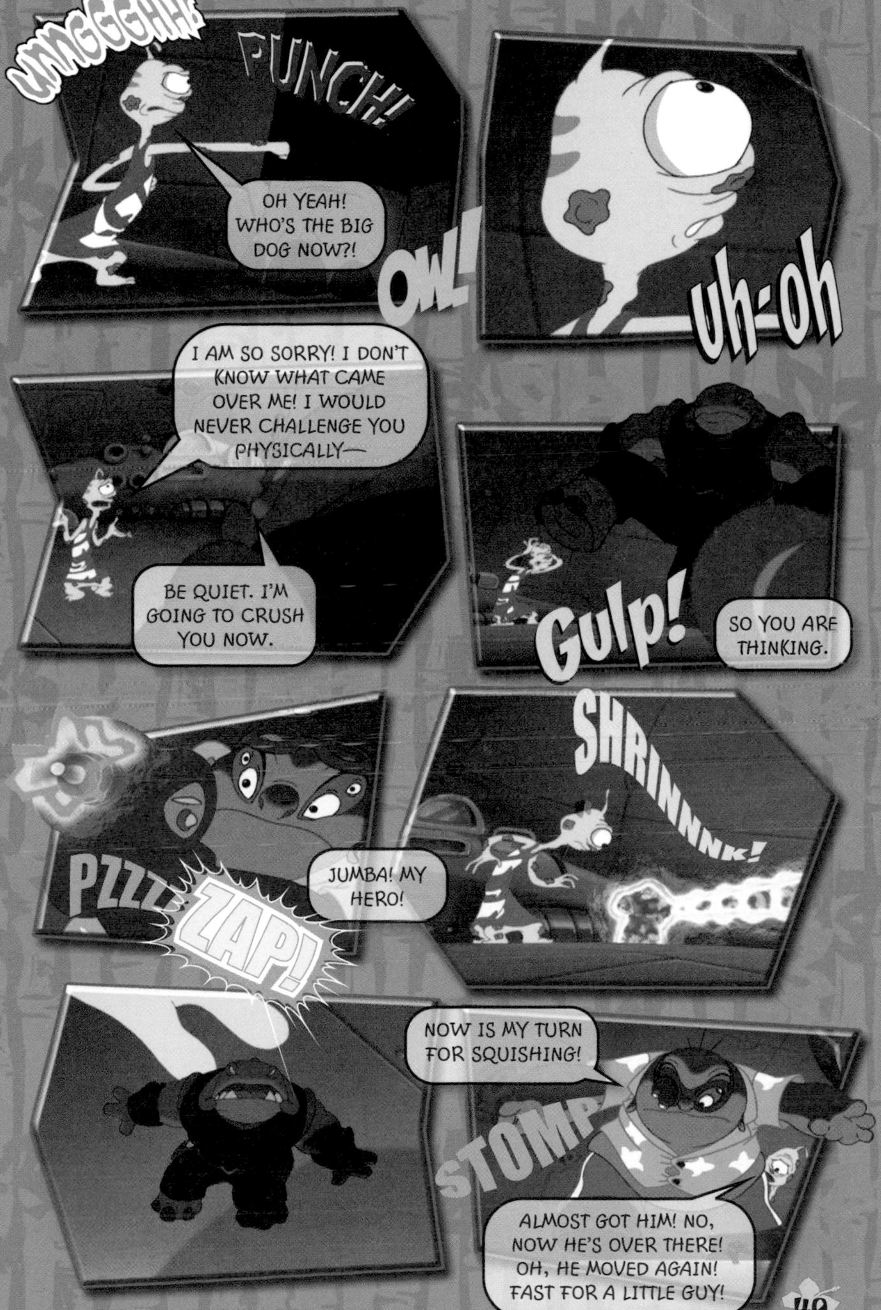
UNNGGGHH!
PUNCH!
OH YEAH! WHO'S THE BIG DOG NOW?!
OW!
uh-oh
I AM SO SORRY! I DON'T KNOW WHAT CAME OVER ME! I WOULD NEVER CHALLENGE YOU PHYSICALLY—
BE QUIET. I'M GOING TO CRUSH YOU NOW.
Gulp!
SO YOU ARE THINKING.
PZZZ
ZAP!
JUMBA! MY HERO!
SHRINNNNK!
NOW IS MY TURN FOR SQUISHING!
STOMP
ALMOST GOT HIM! NO, NOW HE'S OVER THERE! OH, HE MOVED AGAIN! FAST FOR A LITTLE GUY!

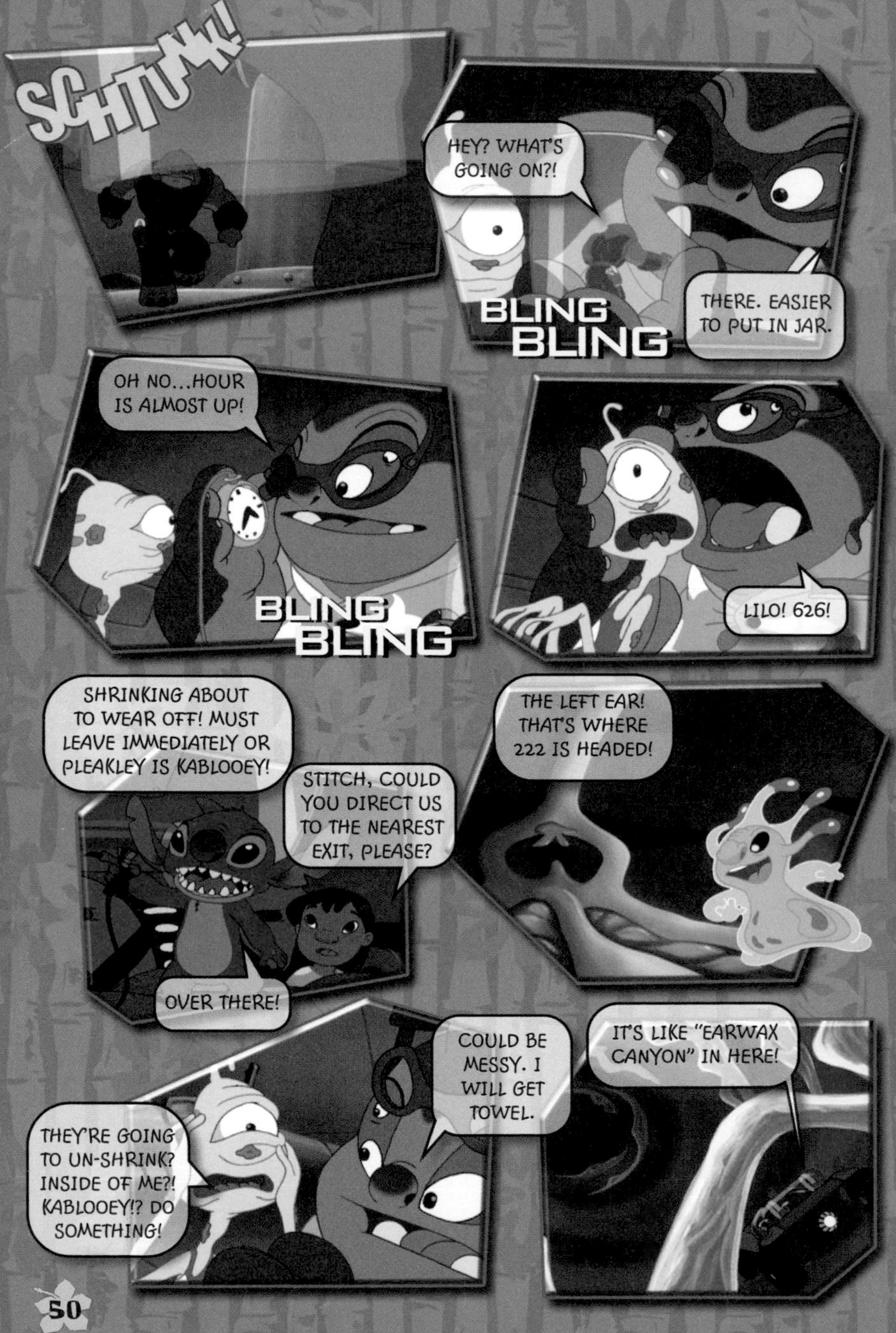
SCHTUNK!
HEY? WHAT'S GOING ON?!
BLING BLING
THERE. EASIER TO PUT IN JAR.
OH NO...HOUR IS ALMOST UP!
BLING BLING
LILO! 626!
SHRINKING ABOUT TO WEAR OFF! MUST LEAVE IMMEDIATELY OR PLEAKLEY IS KABLOOEY!
STITCH, COULD YOU DIRECT US TO THE NEAREST EXIT, PLEASE?
OVER THERE!
THE LEFT EAR! THAT'S WHERE 222 IS HEADED!
THEY'RE GOING TO UN-SHRINK? INSIDE OF ME?! KABLOOEY!? DO SOMETHING!
COULD BE MESSY. I WILL GET TOWEL.
IT'S LIKE "EARWAX CANYON" IN HERE!

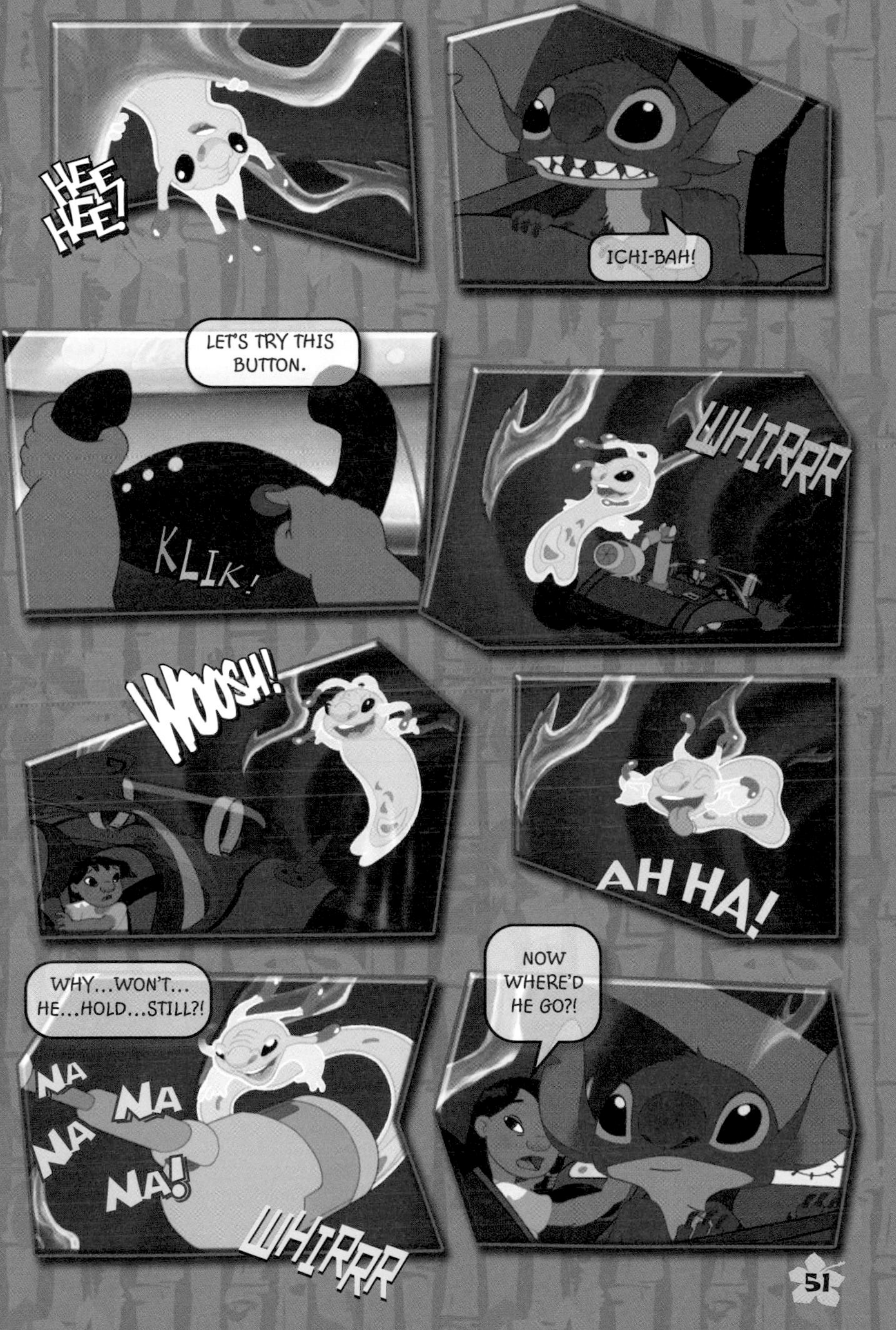
HEE HEE!
ICHI-BAH!
LET'S TRY THIS BUTTON.
KLIK!
WHIRRR
WOOSH!
AH HA!
WHY...WON'T... HE...HOLD...STILL?!
NA NA NA NA!
WHIRRR
NOW WHERE'D HE GO?!

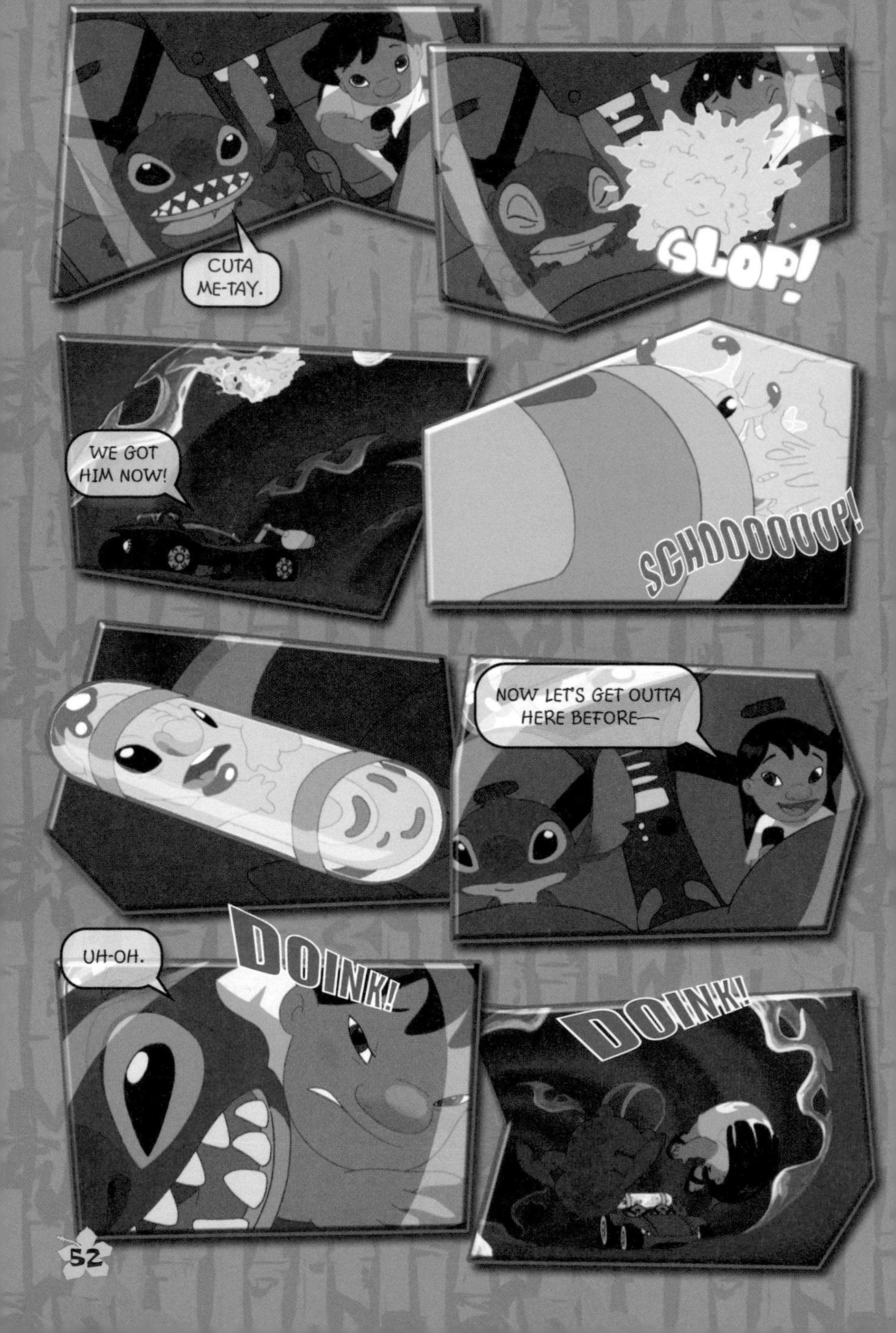

CUTA ME-TAY.
SLOP!
WE GOT HIM NOW!
SCHOOOOOOOP!
NOW LET'S GET OUTTA HERE BEFORE—
UH-OH.
DOINK!
DOINK!

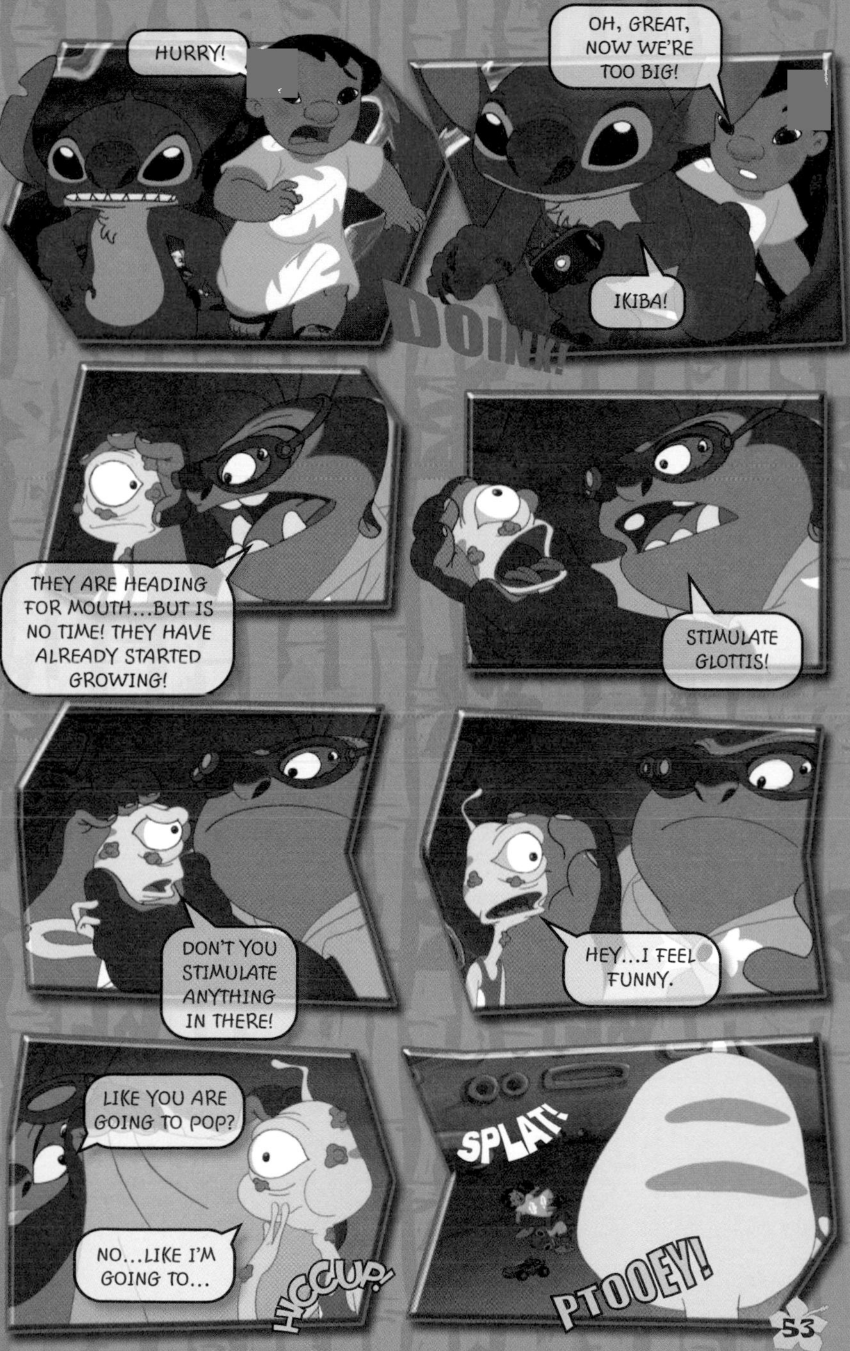
HURRY!
OH, GREAT, NOW WE'RE TOO BIG!
IKIBA!
DOINK!
THEY ARE HEADING FOR MOUTH...BUT IS NO TIME! THEY HAVE ALREADY STARTED GROWING!
STIMULATE GLOTTIS!
DON'T YOU STIMULATE ANYTHING IN THERE!
HEY...I FEEL FUNNY.
LIKE YOU ARE GOING TO POP?
NO...LIKE I'M GOING TO...
HICCUP!
SPLAT!
PTOOEY!

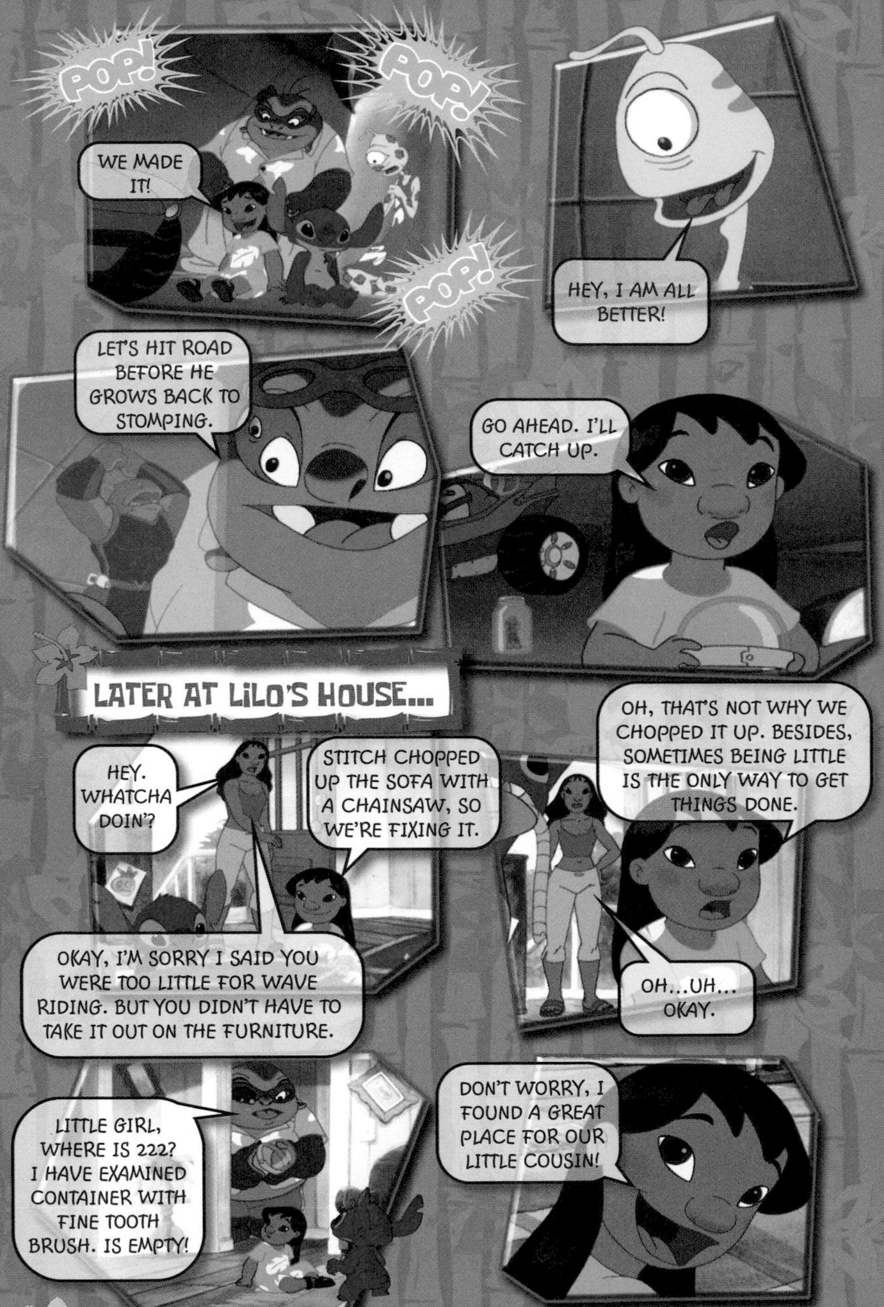
POP!
POP!
WE MADE IT!
POP!
HEY, I AM ALL BETTER!
LET'S HIT ROAD BEFORE HE GROWS BACK TO STOMPING.
GO AHEAD. I'LL CATCH UP.
LATER AT LILO'S HOUSE...
HEY. WHATCHA DOIN'?
STITCH CHOPPED UP THE SOFA WITH A CHAINSAW, SO WE'RE FIXING IT.
OKAY, I'M SORRY I SAID YOU WERE TOO LITTLE FOR WAVE RIDING. BUT YOU DIDN'T HAVE TO TAKE IT OUT ON THE FURNITURE.
OH, THAT'S NOT WHY WE CHOPPED IT UP. BESIDES, SOMETIMES BEING LITTLE IS THE ONLY WAY TO GET THINGS DONE.
OH...UH... OKAY.
LITTLE GIRL, WHERE IS 222? I HAVE EXAMINED CONTAINER WITH FINE TOOTH BRUSH. IS EMPTY!
DON'T WORRY, I FOUND A GREAT PLACE FOR OUR LITTLE COUSIN!

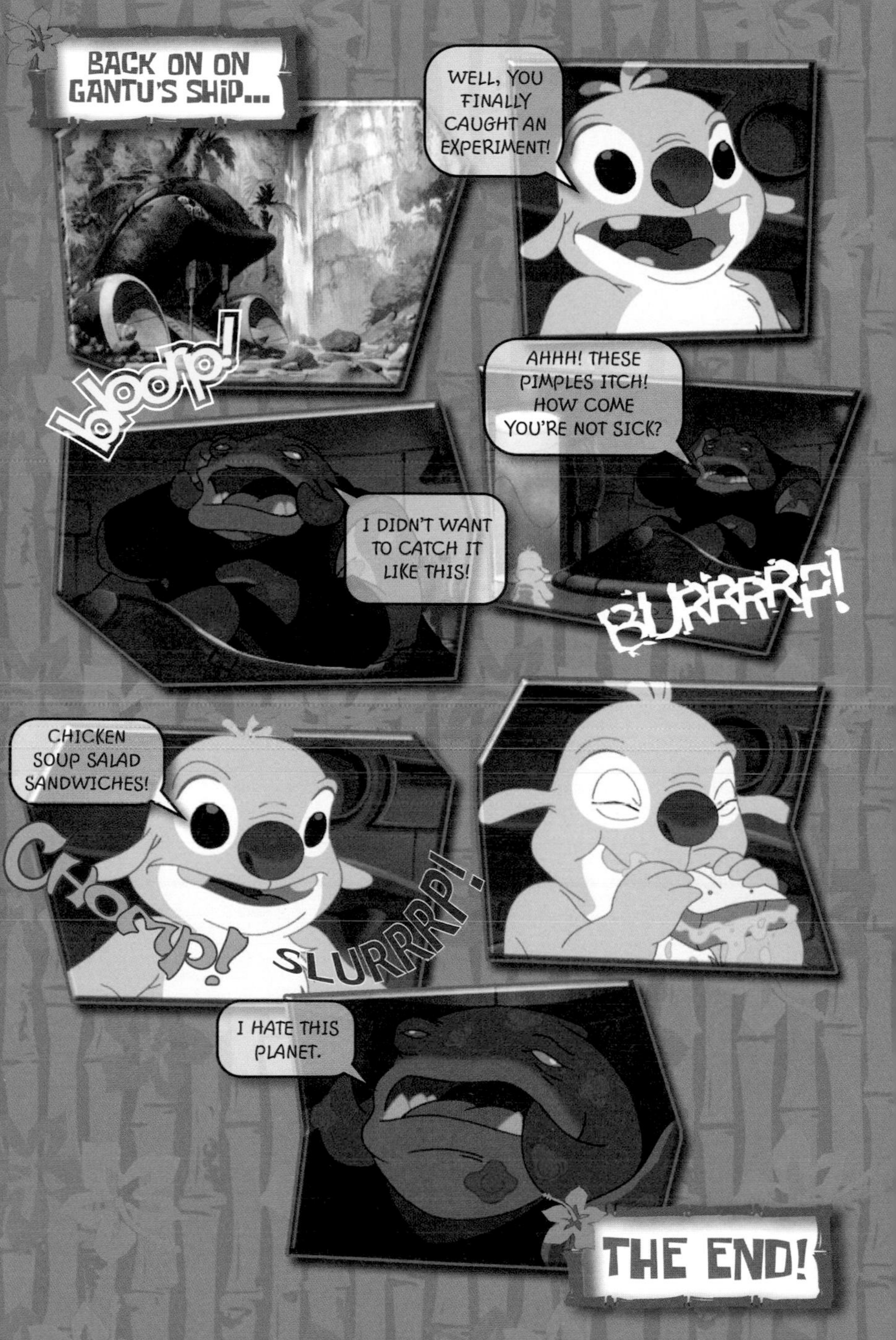
BACK ON ON GANTU'S SHIP...
bloorp!
WELL, YOU FINALLY CAUGHT AN EXPERIMENT!
I DIDN'T WANT TO CATCH IT LIKE THIS!
AHHH! THESE PIMPLES ITCH! HOW COME YOU'RE NOT SICK?
BURRRRP!
CHICKEN SOUP SALAD SANDWICHES!
Chomp!
SLURRRP!
I HATE THIS PLANET.
THE END!

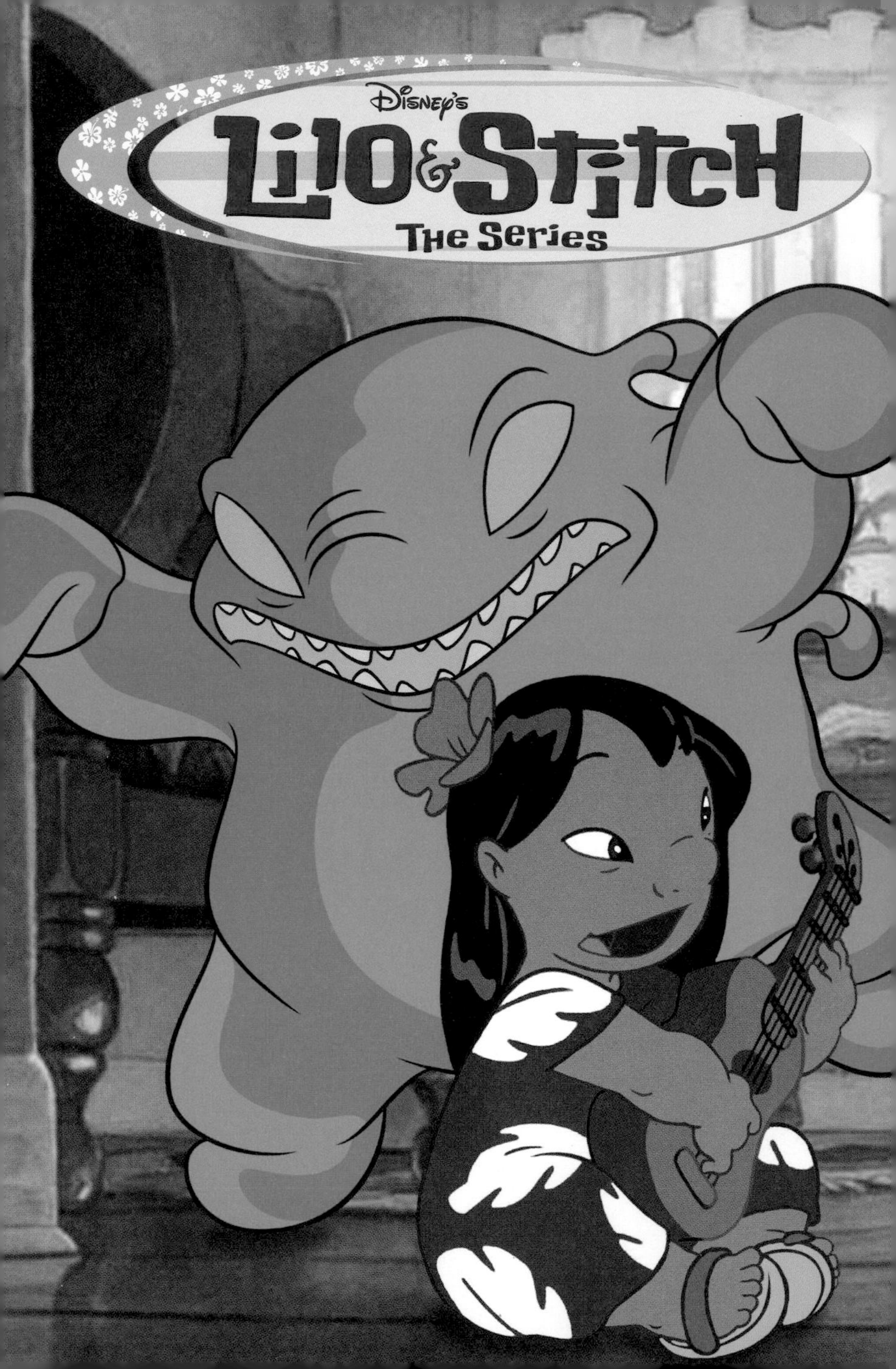
Disney's
Lilo & Stitch
The Series

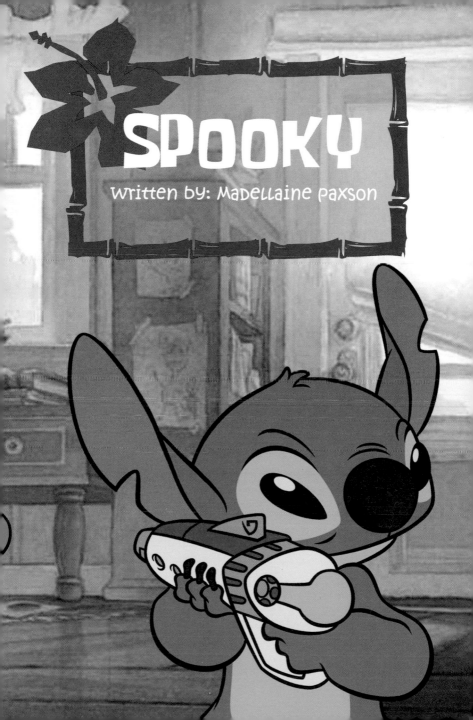

SPOOKY

written by: Madellaine Paxson

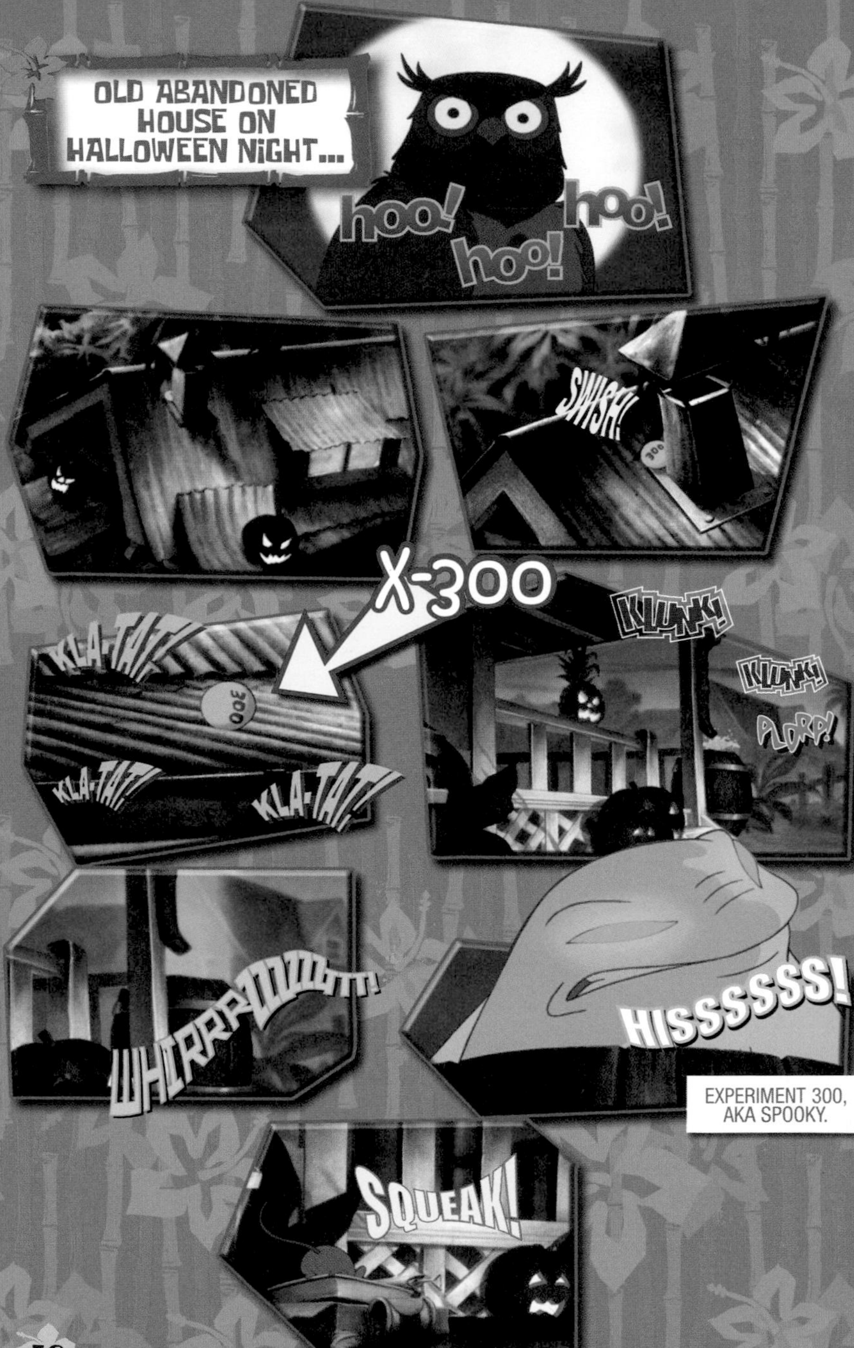

OLD ABANDONED HOUSE ON HALLOWEEN NIGHT...
hoo!
hoo!
hoo!
SWISH!
X-300
KLA-TAT!
KLA-TAT!
KLA-TAT!
KLUNK!
KLUNK!
PLORP!
WHIRRROOOOTTT!
HISSSSSSS!
EXPERIMENT 300, AKA SPOOKY.
SQUEAK!

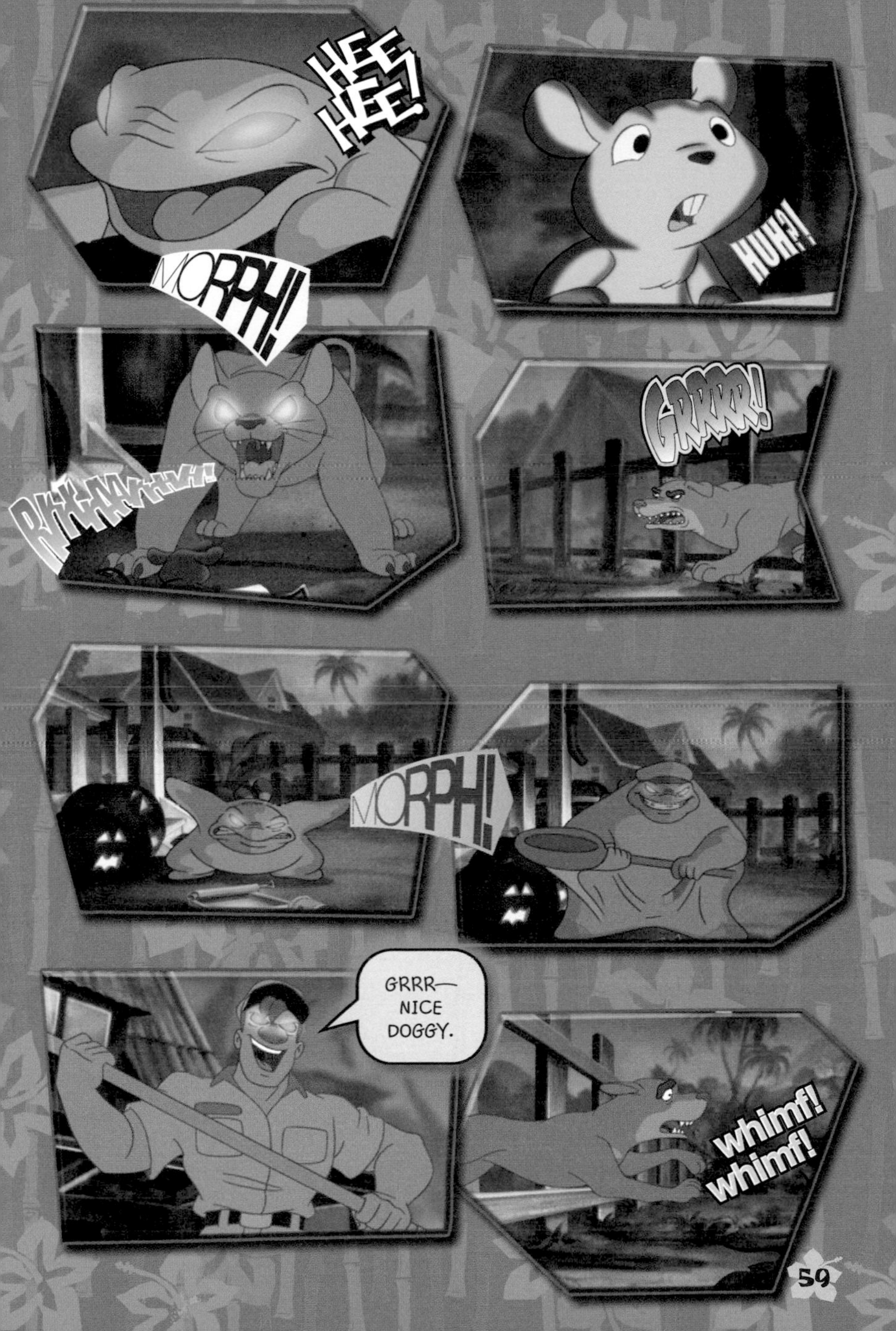
HEE HEE!
MORPH!
HUH?!
GRRRR!
MORPH!
GRRR—
NICE DOGGY.
whimf!
whimf!

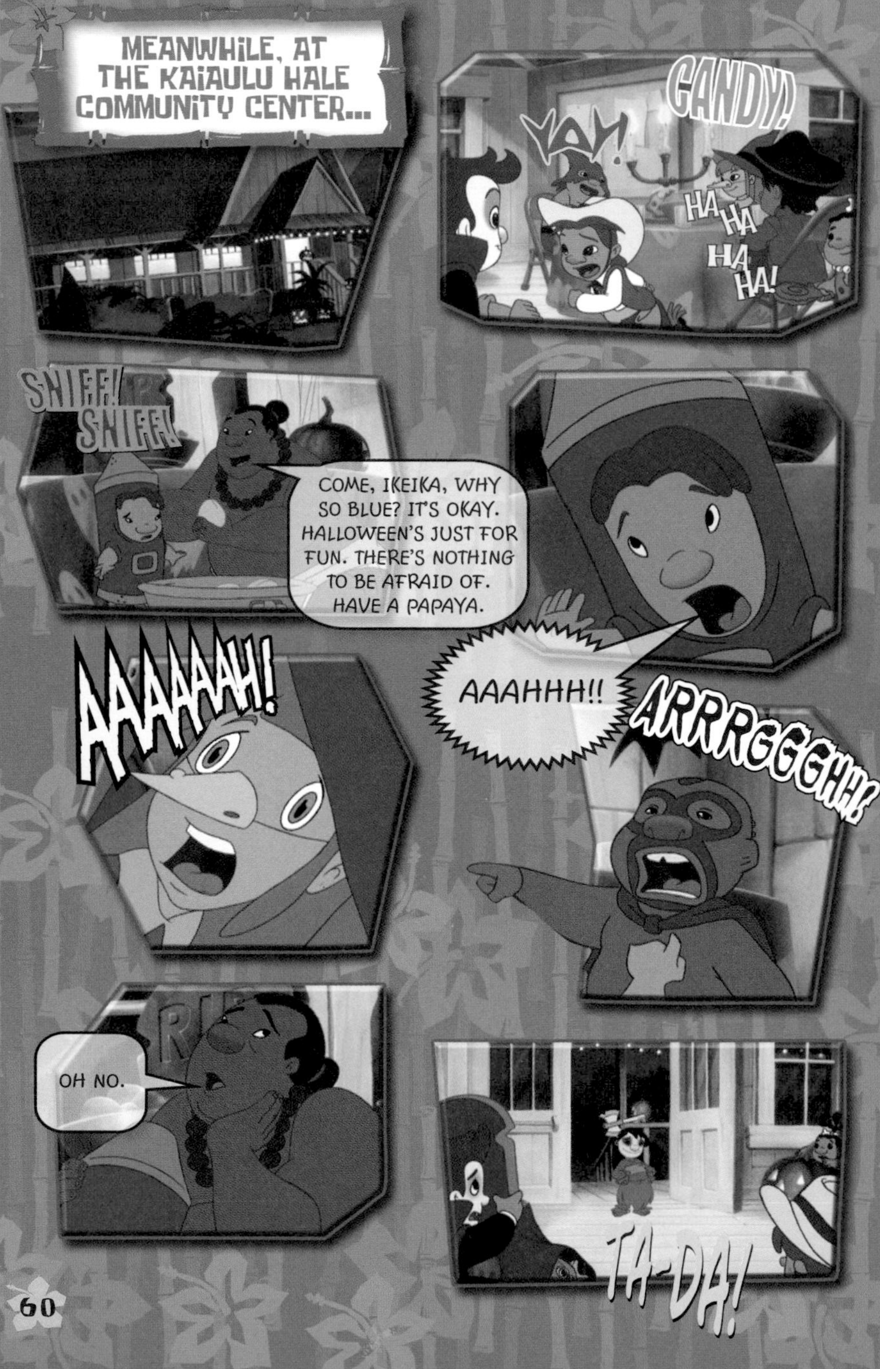
MEANWHILE, AT THE KAIAULU HALE COMMUNITY CENTER...
YAY!
CANDY!
HA HA HA HA!
SNIFF! SNIFF!
COME, IKEIKA, WHY SO BLUE? IT'S OKAY. HALLOWEEN'S JUST FOR FUN. THERE'S NOTHING TO BE AFRAID OF. HAVE A PAPAYA.
AAAHHH!!
AAAAAAH!
ARRRGGGHH!
OH NO.
TA-DA!

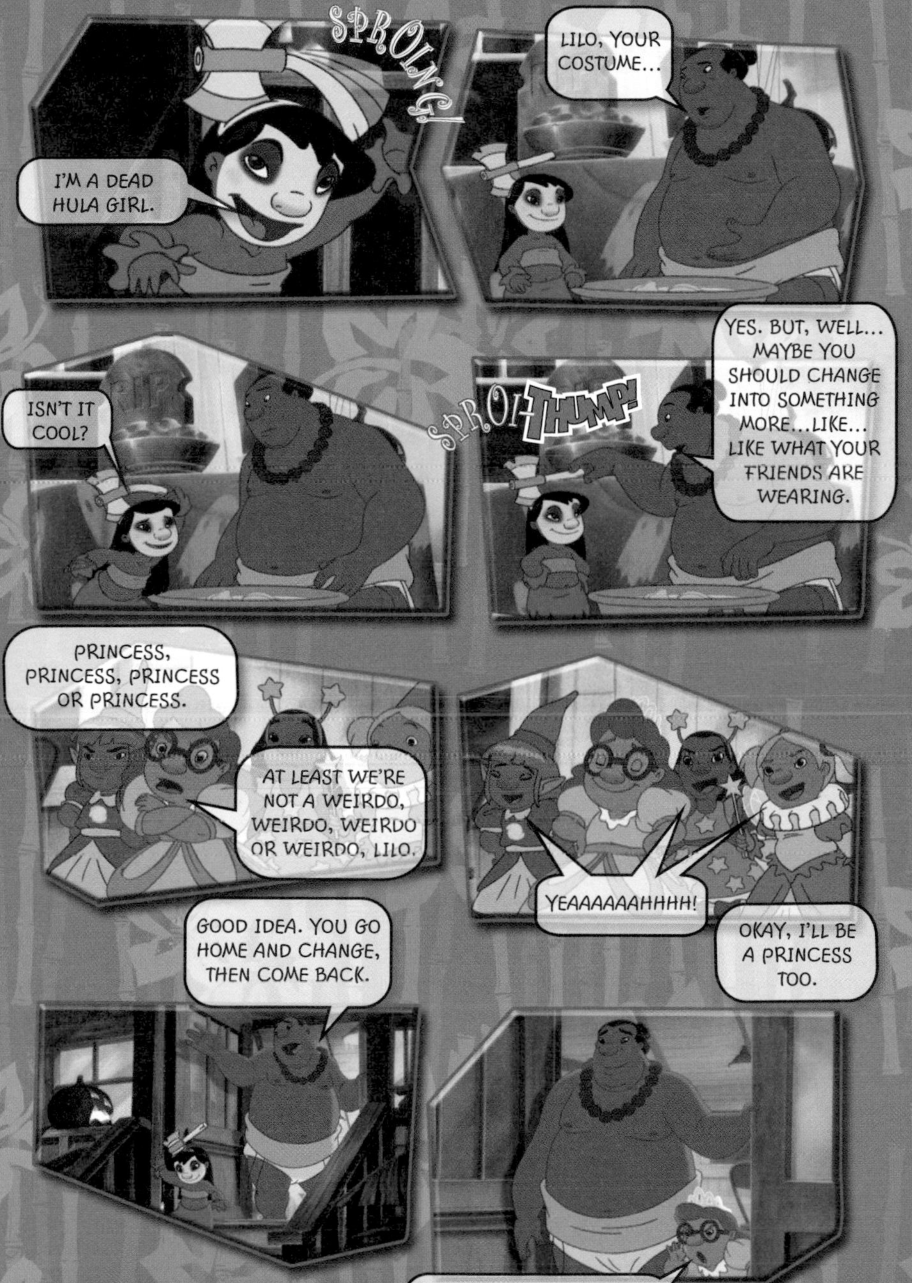
SPROING!
I'M A DEAD HULA GIRL.
LILO, YOUR COSTUME...
ISN'T IT COOL?
SPROI-THUMP!
YES. BUT, WELL... MAYBE YOU SHOULD CHANGE INTO SOMETHING MORE...LIKE... LIKE WHAT YOUR FRIENDS ARE WEARING.
PRINCESS, PRINCESS, PRINCESS OR PRINCESS.
AT LEAST WE'RE NOT A WEIRDO, WEIRDO, WEIRDO OR WEIRDO, LILO.
YEAAAAAAHHHH!
OKAY, I'LL BE A PRINCESS TOO.
GOOD IDEA. YOU GO HOME AND CHANGE, THEN COME BACK.
OR GO HOME, CHANGE, AND DON'T COME BACK.

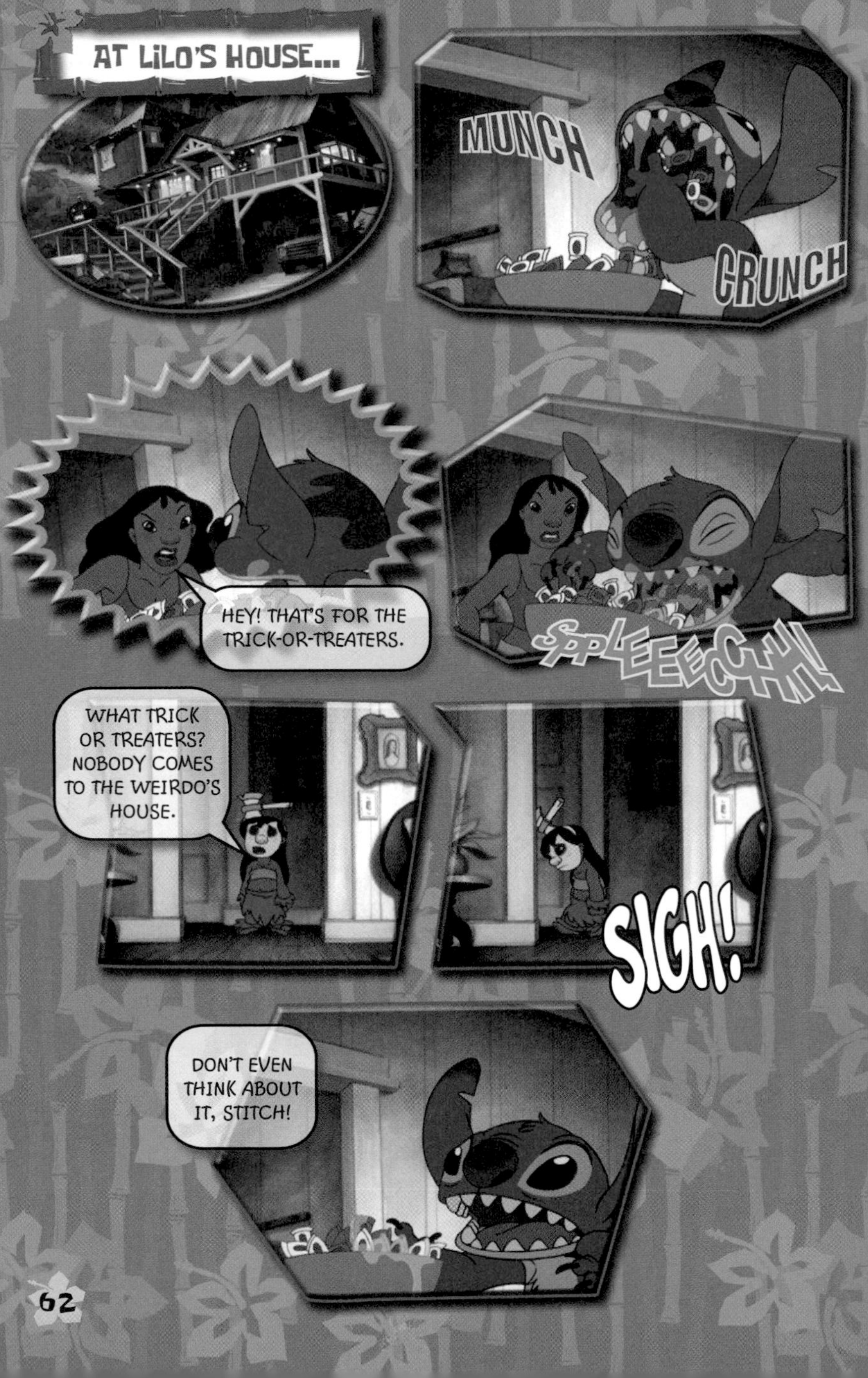
AT LILO'S HOUSE...
MUNCH
CRUNCH
HEY! THAT'S FOR THE TRICK-OR-TREATERS.
SPPLEEECCHH!
WHAT TRICK OR TREATERS? NOBODY COMES TO THE WEIRDO'S HOUSE.
SIGH!
DON'T EVEN THINK ABOUT IT, STITCH!

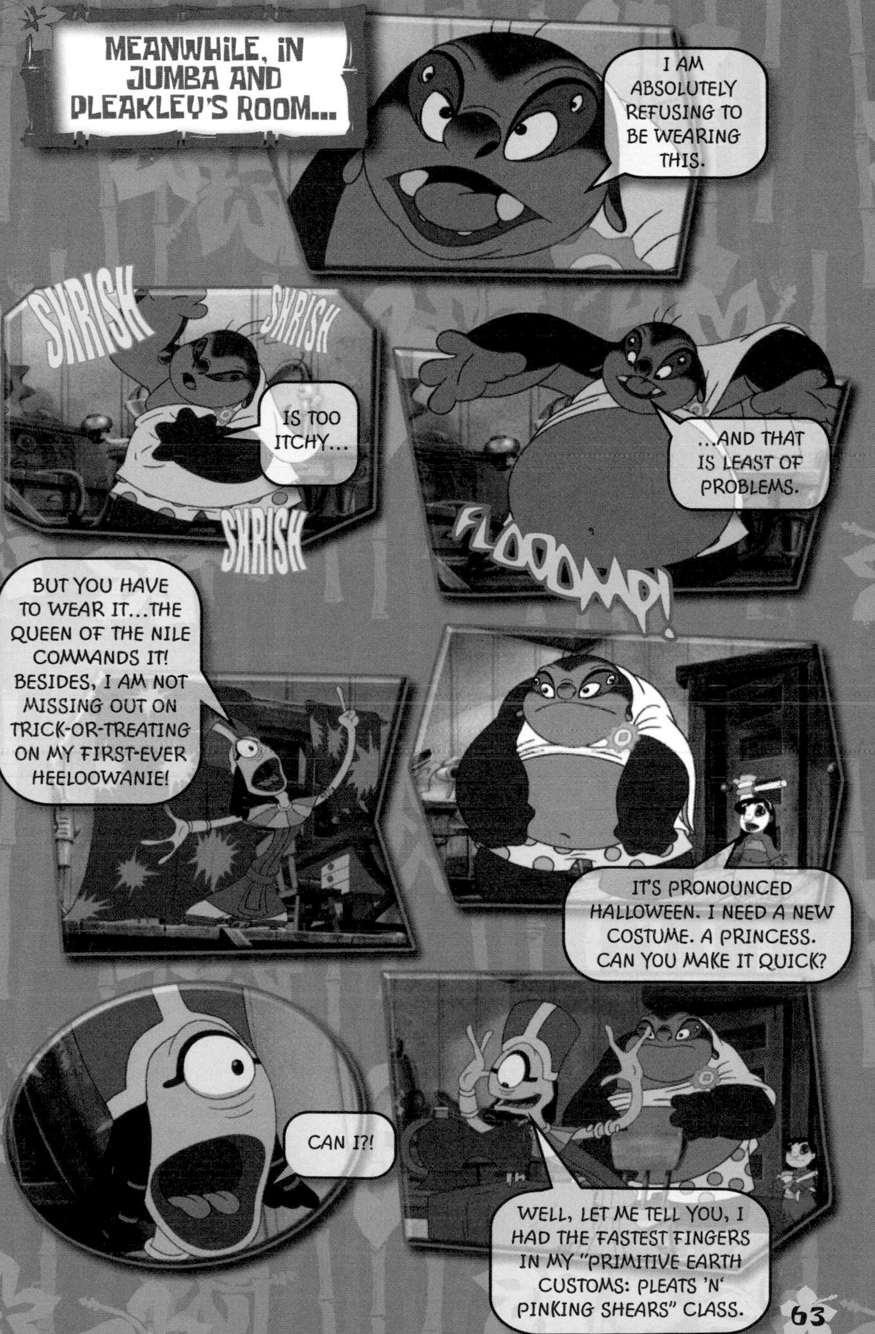
MEANWHILE, IN JUMBA AND PLEAKLEY'S ROOM...
I AM ABSOLUTELY REFUSING TO BE WEARING THIS.
SHRISH
SHRISH
IS TOO ITCHY...
SHRISH
...AND THAT IS LEAST OF PROBLEMS.
FLOOOMP!
BUT YOU HAVE TO WEAR IT...THE QUEEN OF THE NILE COMMANDS IT! BESIDES, I AM NOT MISSING OUT ON TRICK-OR-TREATING ON MY FIRST-EVER HEELOOWANIE!
IT'S PRONOUNCED HALLOWEEN. I NEED A NEW COSTUME. A PRINCESS. CAN YOU MAKE IT QUICK?
CAN I?!
WELL, LET ME TELL YOU, I HAD THE FASTEST FINGERS IN MY "PRIMITIVE EARTH CUSTOMS: PLEATS 'N' PINKING SHEARS" CLASS.

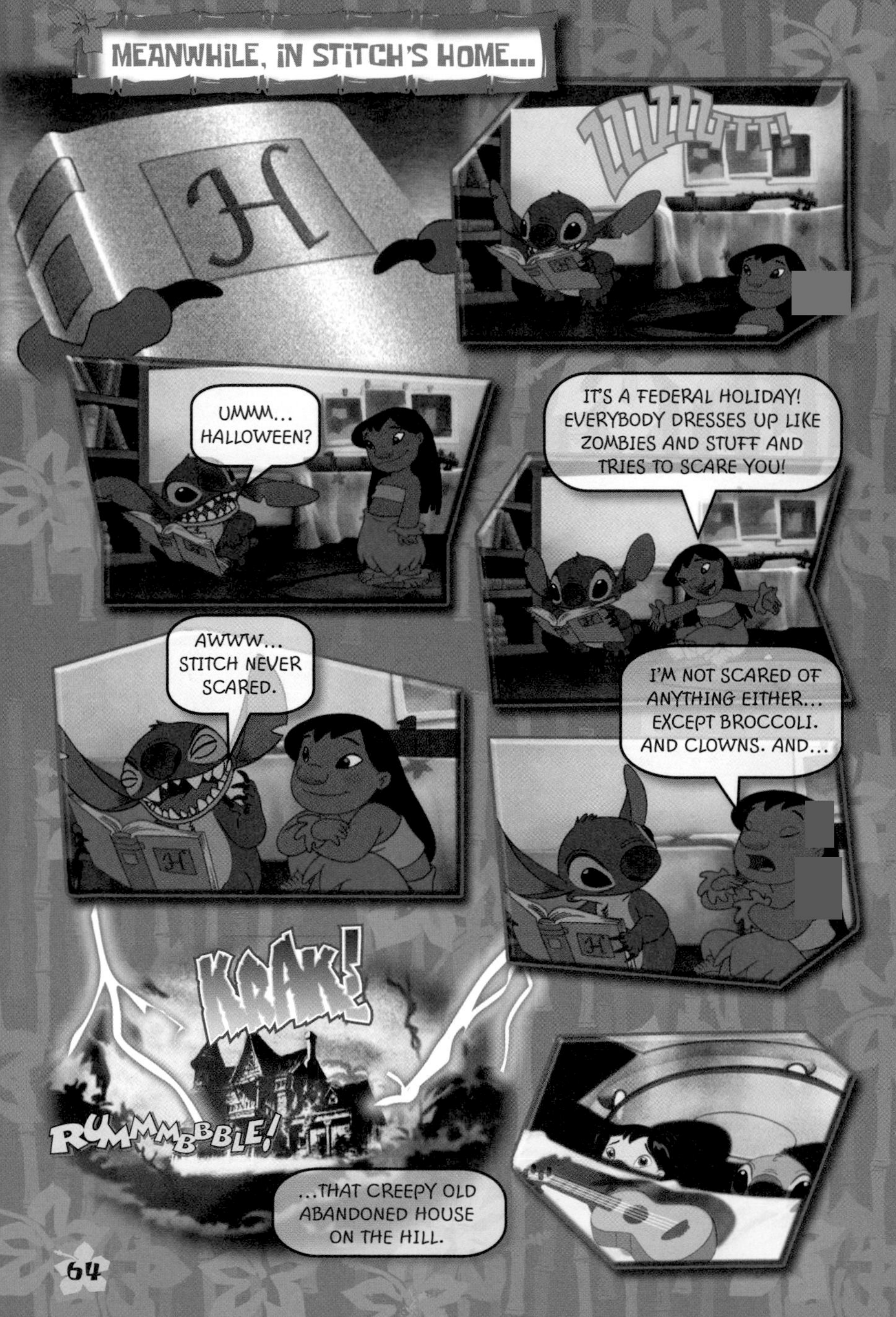
MEANWHILE, IN STITCH'S HOME...
ZZZZZZTTT!
UMMM... HALLOWEEN?
IT'S A FEDERAL HOLIDAY! EVERYBODY DRESSES UP LIKE ZOMBIES AND STUFF AND TRIES TO SCARE YOU!
AWWW... STITCH NEVER SCARED.
I'M NOT SCARED OF ANYTHING EITHER... EXCEPT BROCCOLI. AND CLOWNS. AND...
KRAK!
RUMMMBBBLE!
...THAT CREEPY OLD ABANDONED HOUSE ON THE HILL.

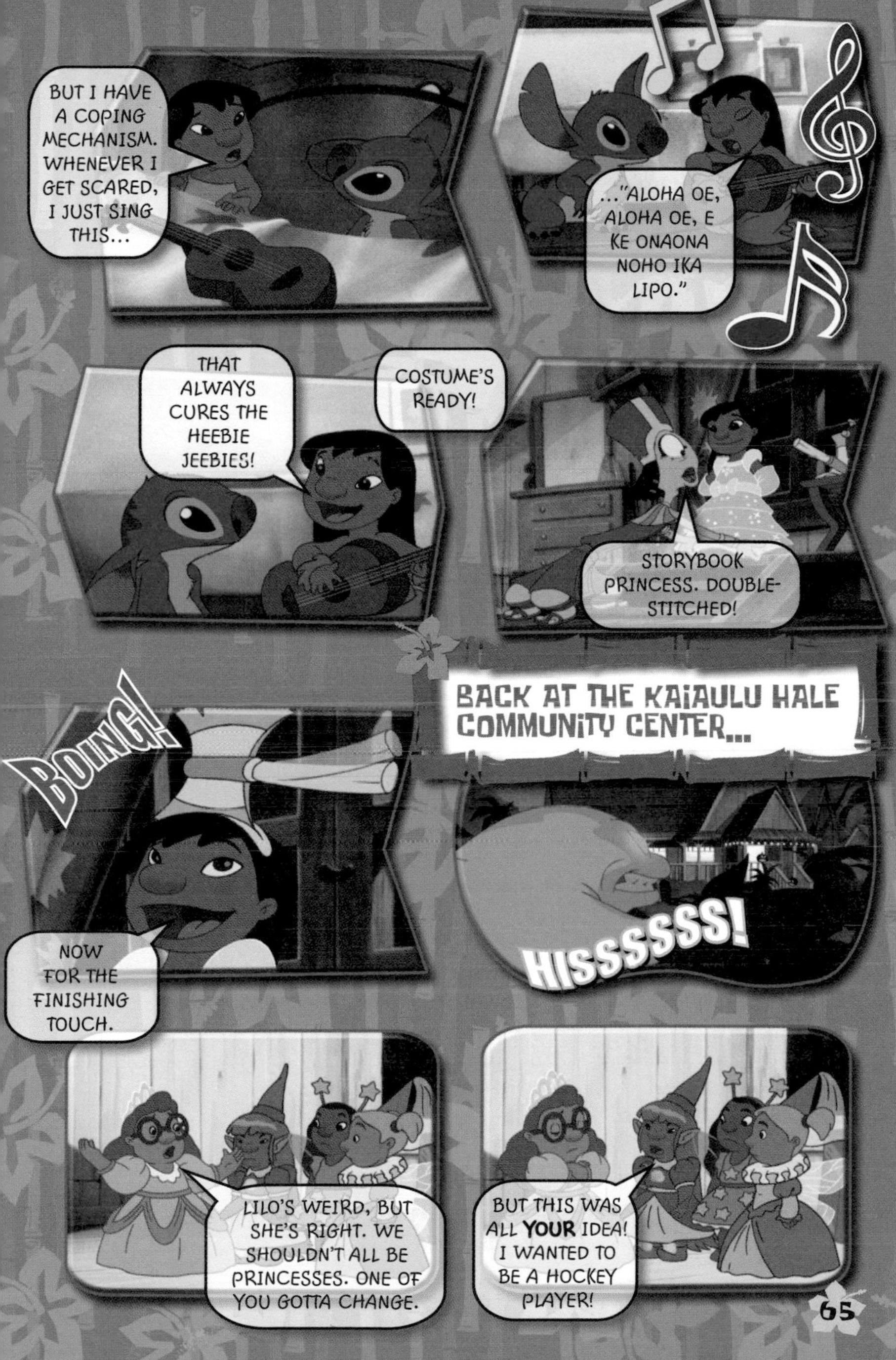
BUT I HAVE A COPING MECHANISM. WHENEVER I GET SCARED, I JUST SING THIS...
..."ALOHA OE, ALOHA OE, E KE ONAONA NOHO IKA LIPO."
THAT ALWAYS CURES THE HEEBIE JEEBIES!
COSTUME'S READY!
STORYBOOK PRINCESS. DOUBLE-STITCHED!
BOING!
NOW FOR THE FINISHING TOUCH.
BACK AT THE KAIAULU HALE COMMUNITY CENTER...
HISSSSSS!
LILO'S WEIRD, BUT SHE'S RIGHT. WE SHOULDN'T ALL BE PRINCESSES. ONE OF YOU GOTTA CHANGE.
BUT THIS WAS ALL **YOUR** IDEA! I WANTED TO BE A HOCKEY PLAYER!

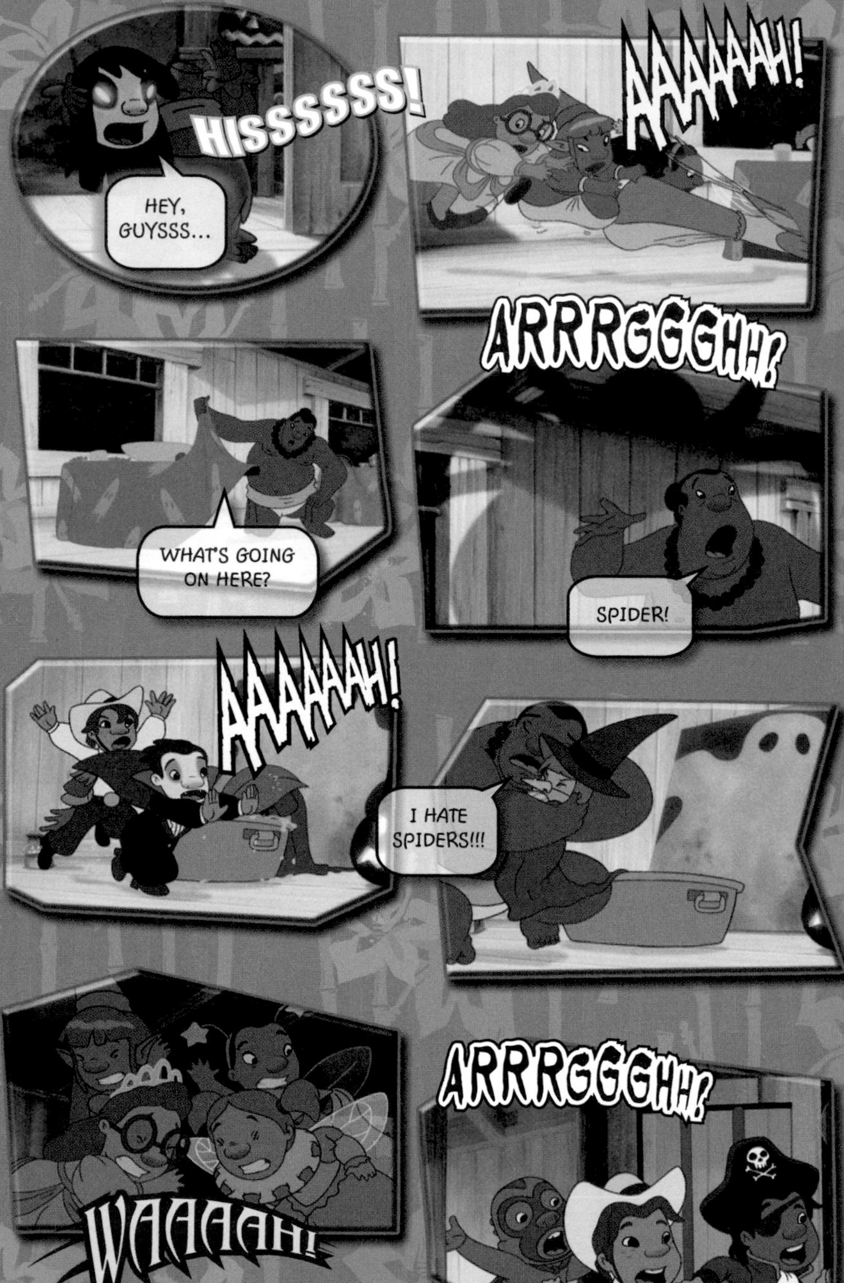
HISSSSSS!
HEY, GUYSSS...
AAAAAAH!
WHAT'S GOING ON HERE?
ARRRGGGHH!
SPIDER!
AAAAAAH!
I HATE SPIDERS!!!
WAAAAH!
ARRRGGGHH!

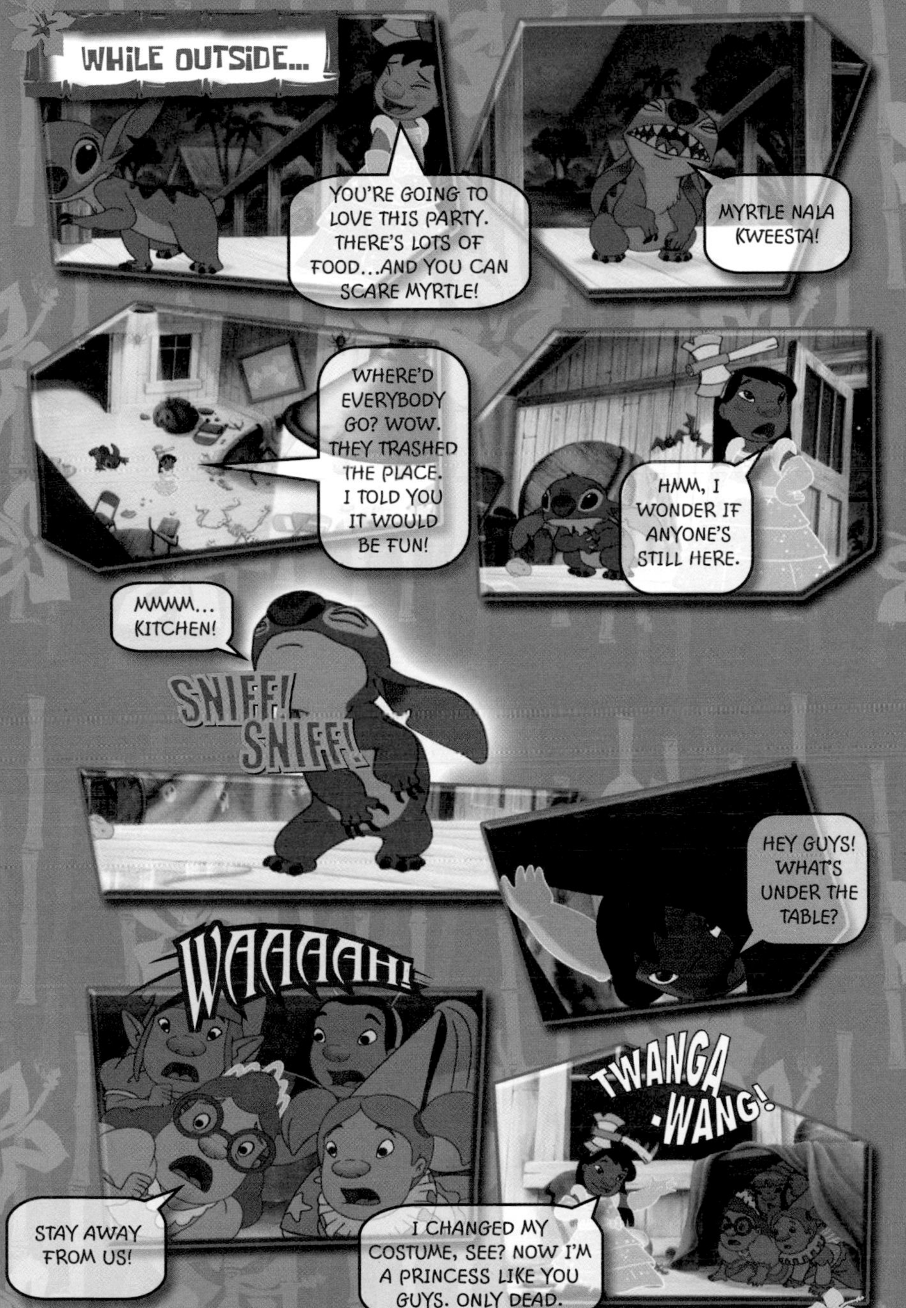
WHILE OUTSIDE...
YOU'RE GOING TO LOVE THIS PARTY. THERE'S LOTS OF FOOD...AND YOU CAN SCARE MYRTLE!
MYRTLE NALA KWEESTA!
WHERE'D EVERYBODY GO? WOW. THEY TRASHED THE PLACE. I TOLD YOU IT WOULD BE FUN!
HMM, I WONDER IF ANYONE'S STILL HERE.
MMMM... KITCHEN!
SNIFF! SNIFF!
HEY GUYS! WHAT'S UNDER THE TABLE?
WAAAAH!
STAY AWAY FROM US!
TWANGA-WANG!
I CHANGED MY COSTUME, SEE? NOW I'M A PRINCESS LIKE YOU GUYS. ONLY DEAD.

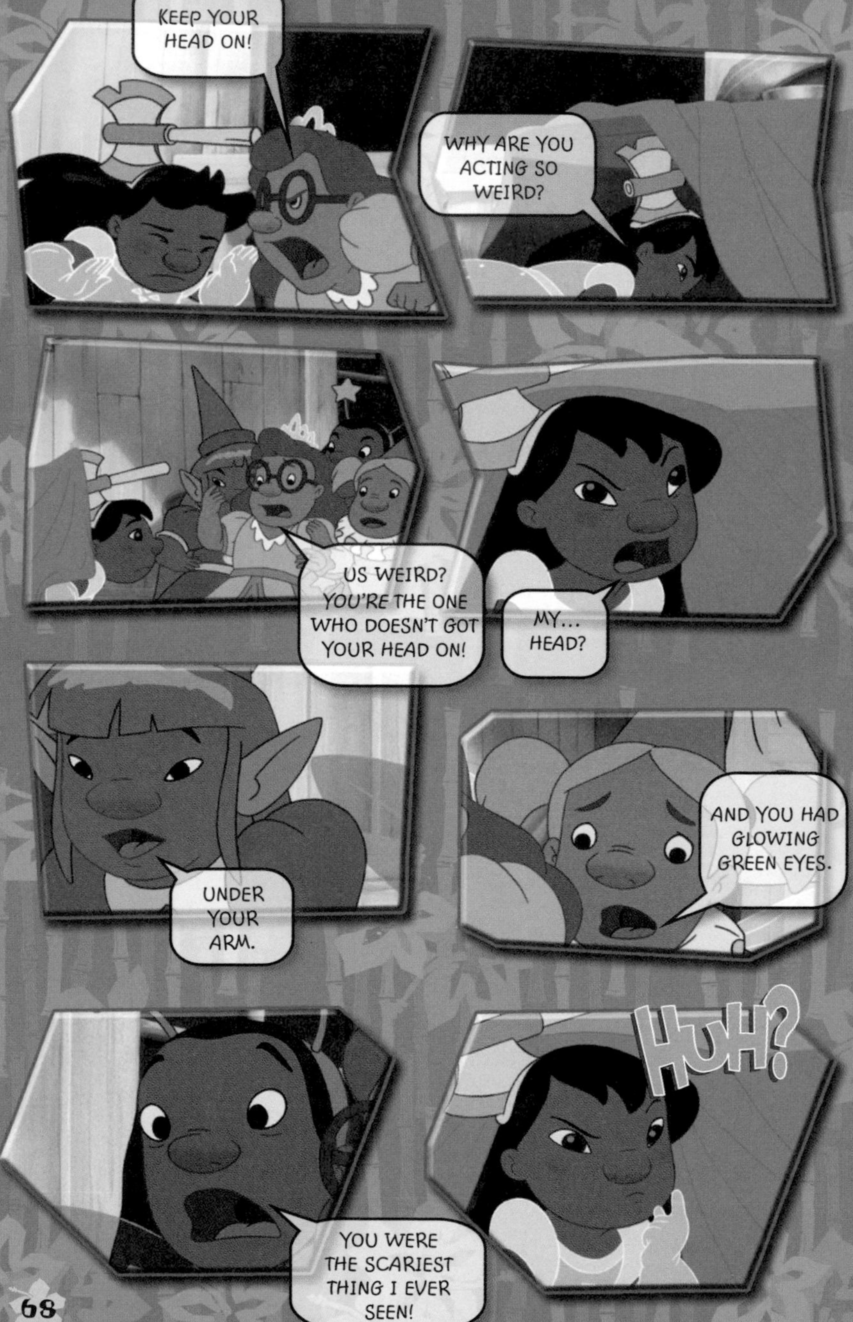
KEEP YOUR HEAD ON!
WHY ARE YOU ACTING SO WEIRD?
US WEIRD? *YOU'RE* THE ONE WHO DOESN'T GOT YOUR HEAD ON!
MY... HEAD?
UNDER YOUR ARM.
AND YOU HAD GLOWING GREEN EYES.
YOU WERE THE SCARIEST THING I EVER SEEN!
HUH?

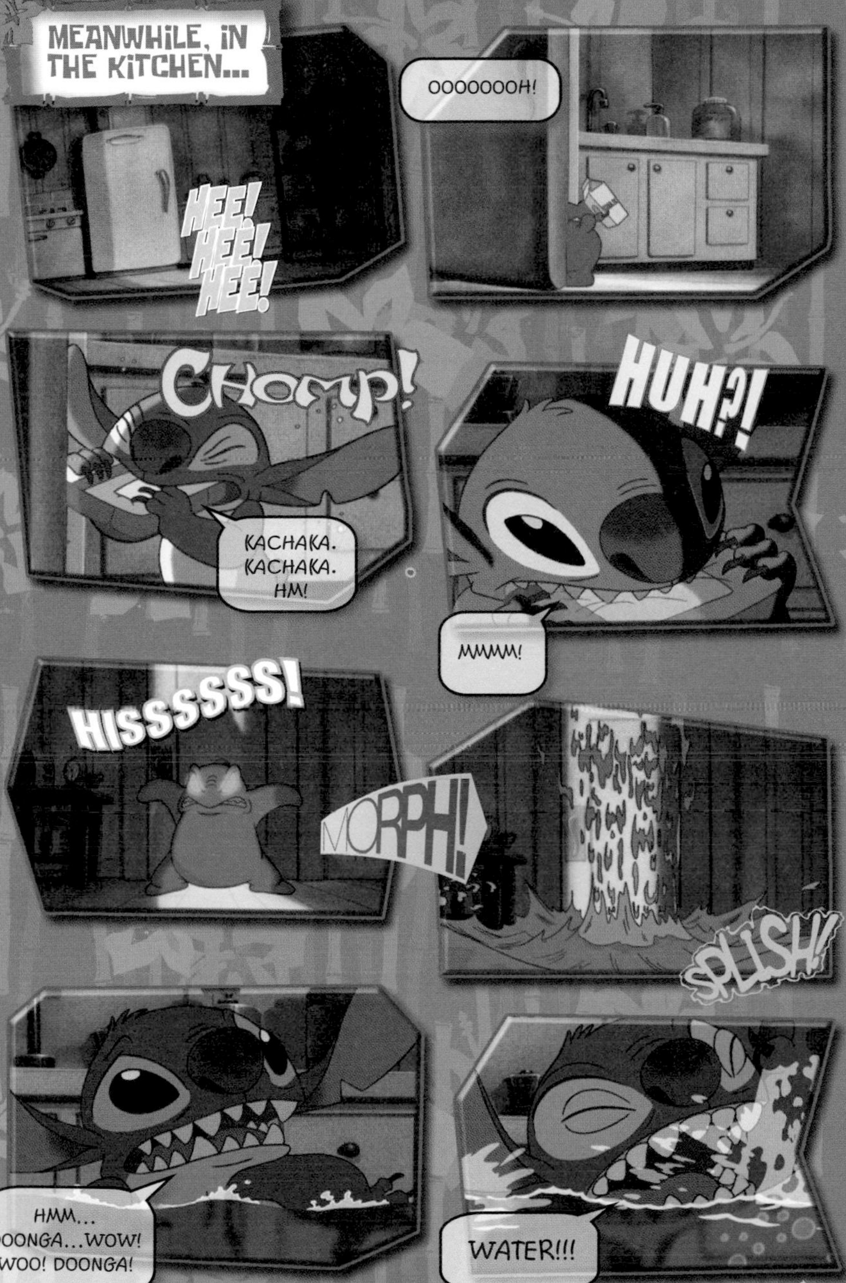

MEANWHILE, IN THE KITCHEN...
HEE! HEE! HEE!
OOOOOOOH!
CHOMP!
KACHAKA. KACHAKA. HM!
HUH?!
MMMM!
HISSSSSSS!
MORPH!
SPLISH!
HMM... DOONGA...WOW! WOO! DOONGA!
WATER!!!

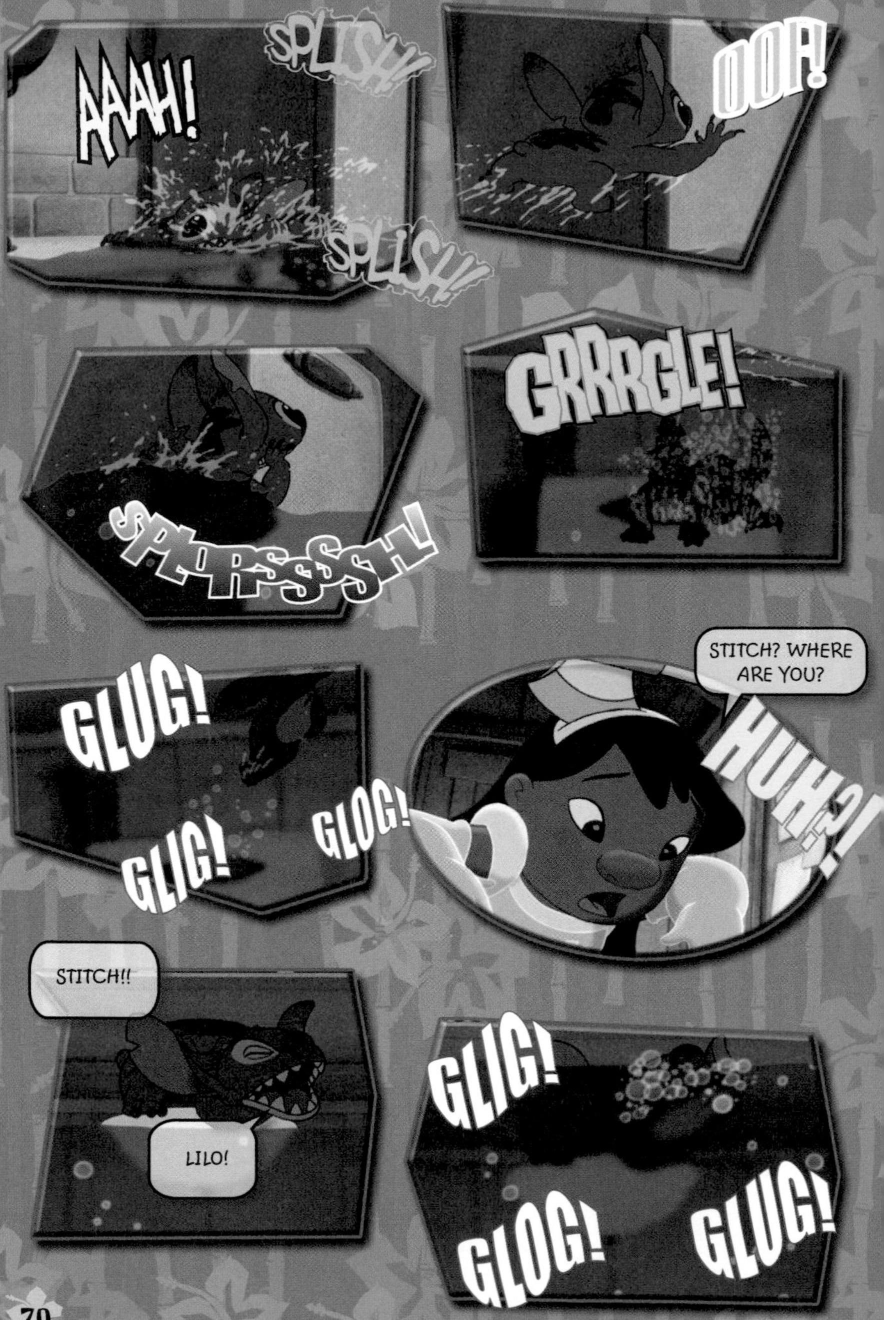
AAAH!
SPLISH!
SPLISH!
OOF!
SPLORSSSSH!
GRRRGLE!
GLUG!
GLIG!
GLOG!
STITCH? WHERE ARE YOU?
HUH?!
STITCH!!
LILO!
GLIG!
GLOG!
GLUG!

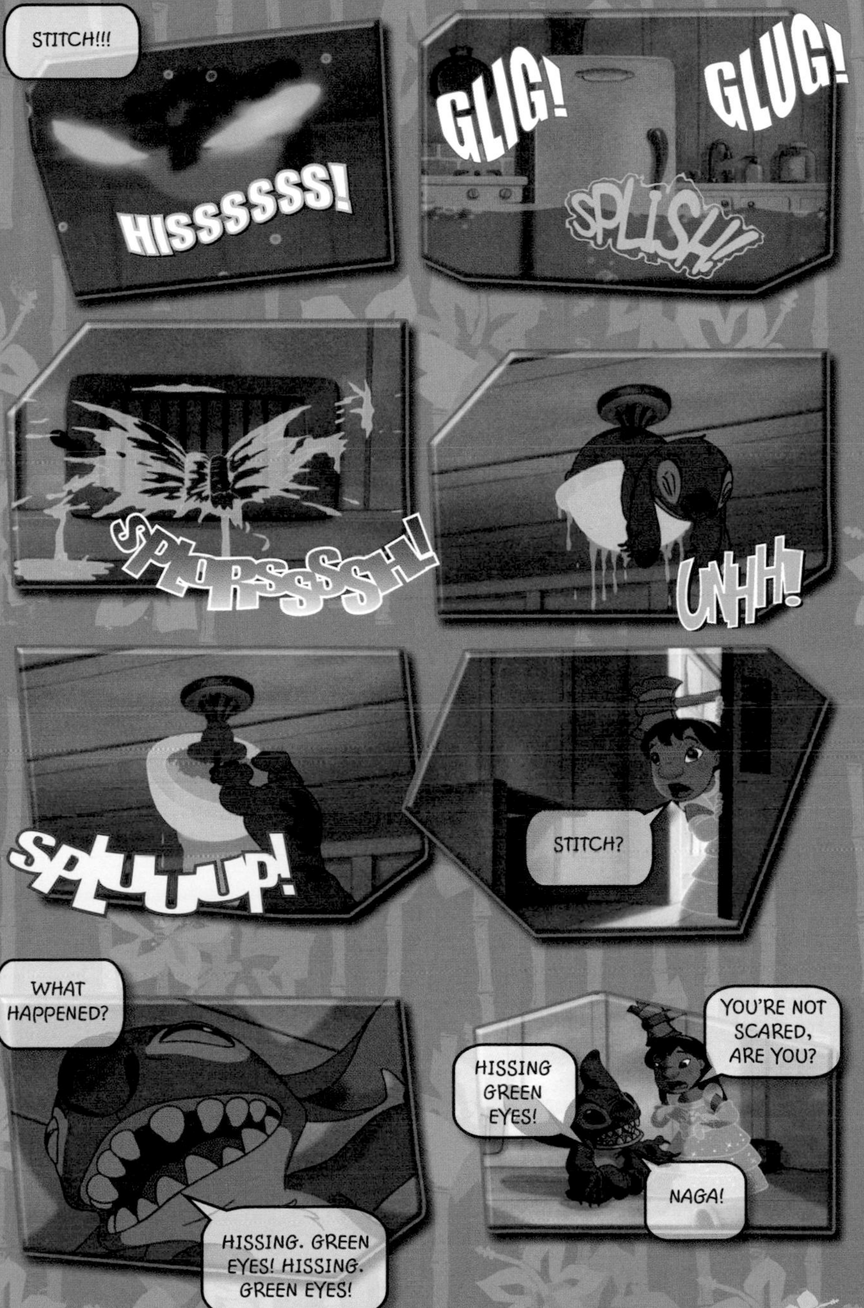
STITCH!!!
HISSSSSS!
GLIG!
GLUG!
SPLISH!!
SPLURSSSSH!
UNHH!
SPLUUUP!
STITCH?
WHAT HAPPENED?
HISSING. GREEN EYES! HISSING. GREEN EYES!
HISSING GREEN EYES!
YOU'RE NOT SCARED, ARE YOU?
NAGA!

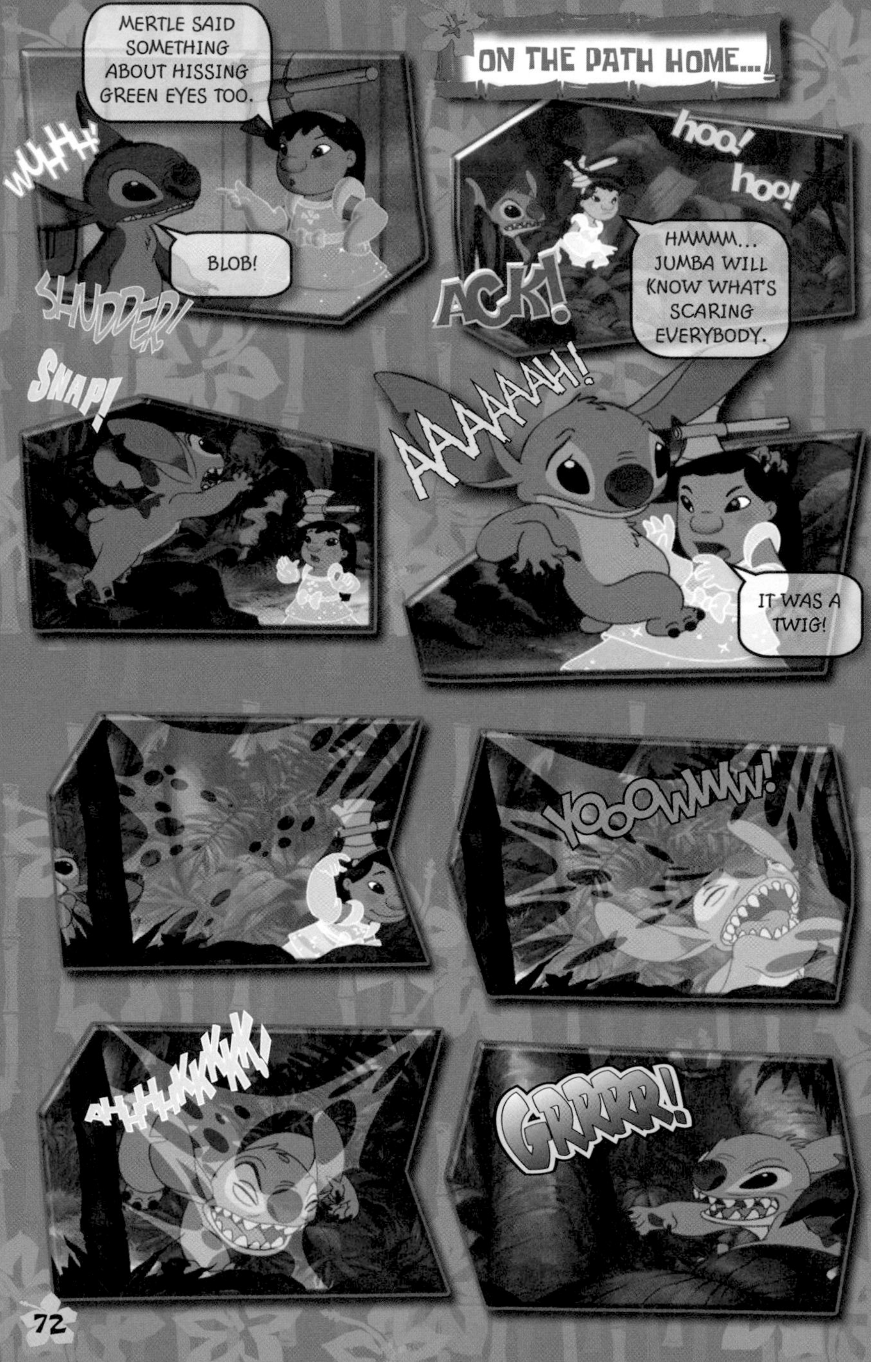
MERTLE SAID SOMETHING ABOUT HISSING GREEN EYES TOO.
BLOB!
SHUDDER!
ON THE PATH HOME...
hoo!
hoo!
ACK!
HMMMM... JUMBA WILL KNOW WHAT'S SCARING EVERYBODY.
SNAP!
AAAAAAH!
IT WAS A TWIG!
GRRRR!

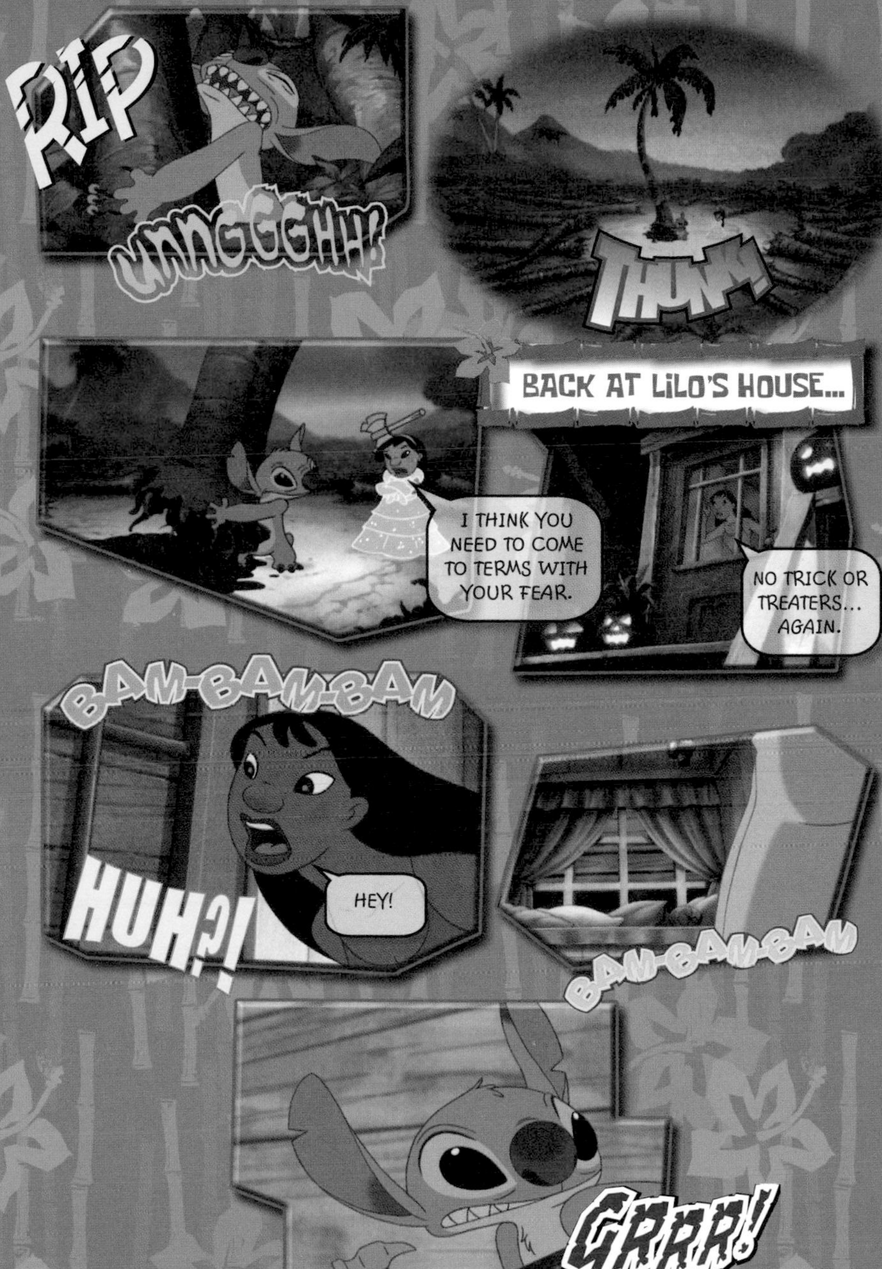
RIP
UNNGGGHH!
THUNK!
I THINK YOU NEED TO COME TO TERMS WITH YOUR FEAR.
BACK AT LILO'S HOUSE...
NO TRICK OR TREATERS... AGAIN.
BAM-BAM-BAM
HUH?!
HEY!
BAM-BAM-BAM
GRRR!

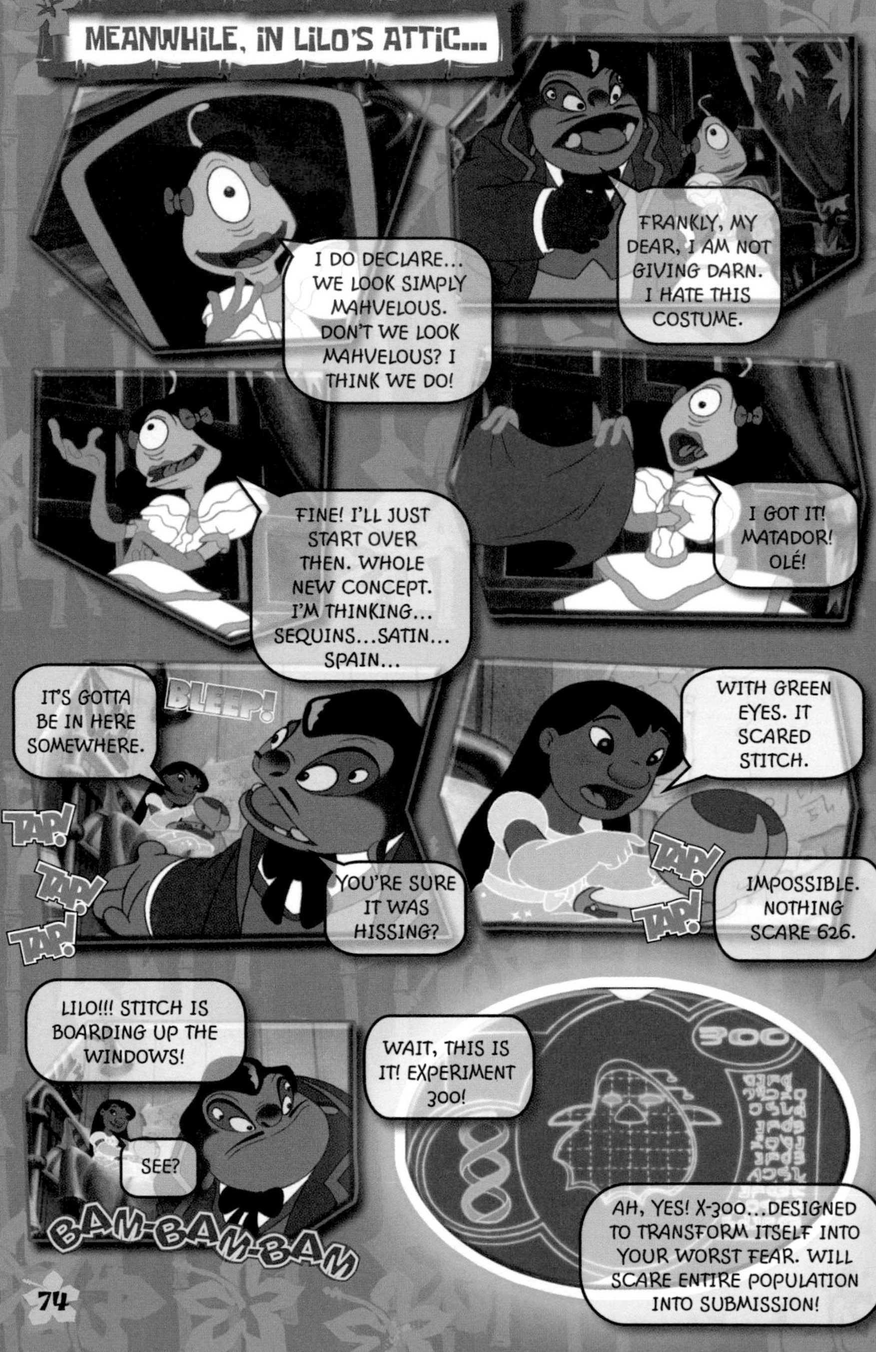
MEANWHILE, IN LILO'S ATTIC...
I DO DECLARE... WE LOOK SIMPLY MAHVELOUS. DON'T WE LOOK MAHVELOUS? I THINK WE DO!
FRANKLY, MY DEAR, I AM NOT GIVING DARN. I HATE THIS COSTUME.
FINE! I'LL JUST START OVER THEN. WHOLE NEW CONCEPT. I'M THINKING... SEQUINS...SATIN... SPAIN...
I GOT IT! MATADOR! OLÉ!
IT'S GOTTA BE IN HERE SOMEWHERE.
BLEEP!
TAP! TAP! TAP!
YOU'RE SURE IT WAS HISSING?
WITH GREEN EYES. IT SCARED STITCH.
TAP! TAP!
IMPOSSIBLE. NOTHING SCARE 626.
LILO!!! STITCH IS BOARDING UP THE WINDOWS!
SEE?
BAM-BAM-BAM
WAIT, THIS IS IT! EXPERIMENT 300!
300
AH, YES! X-300...DESIGNED TO TRANSFORM ITSELF INTO YOUR WORST FEAR. WILL SCARE ENTIRE POPULATION INTO SUBMISSION!

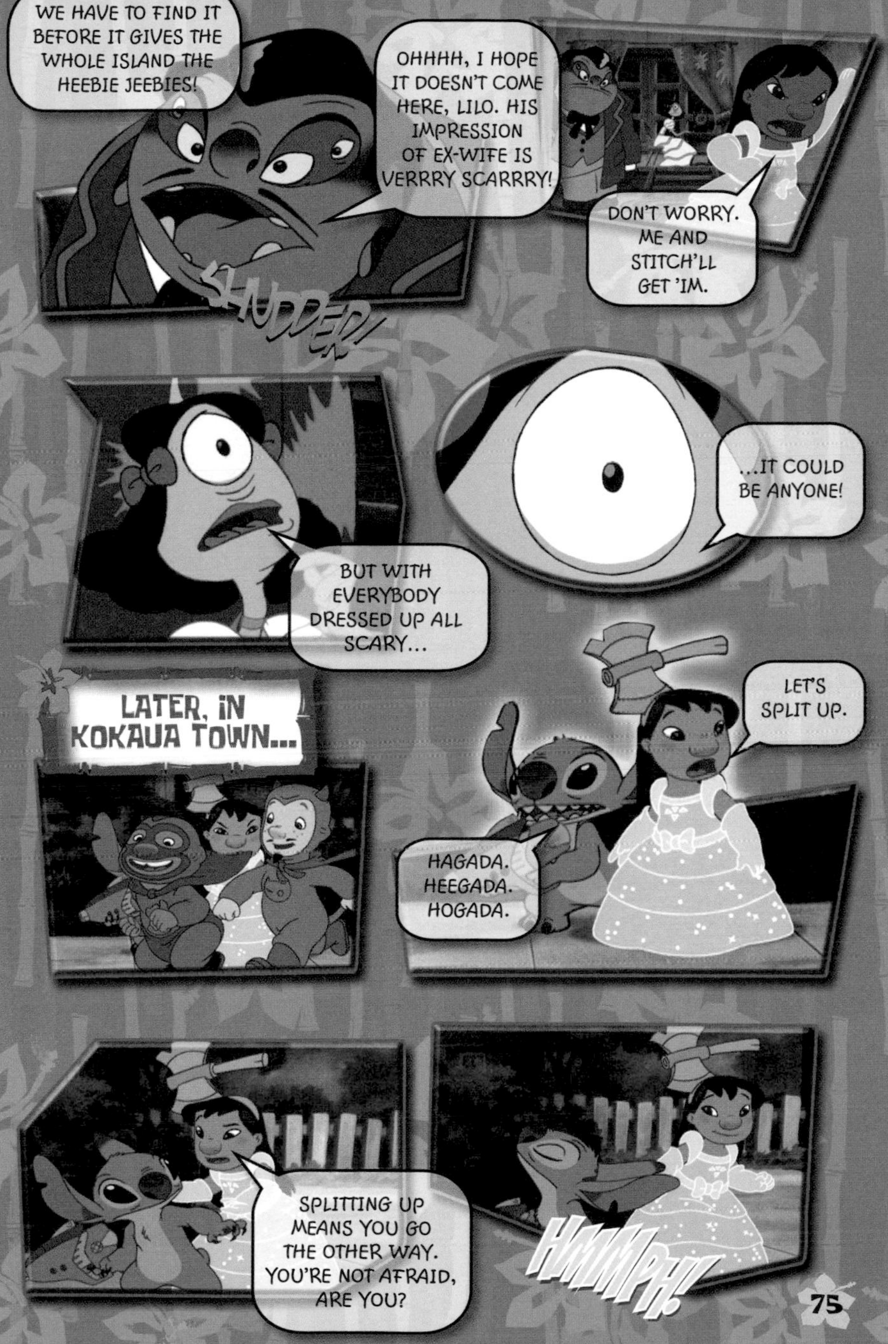

WE HAVE TO FIND IT BEFORE IT GIVES THE WHOLE ISLAND THE HEEBIE JEEBIES!
OHHHH, I HOPE IT DOESN'T COME HERE, LILO. HIS IMPRESSION OF EX-WIFE IS VERRRY SCARRRY!
SHUDDER!
DON'T WORRY. ME AND STITCH'LL GET 'IM.
BUT WITH EVERYBODY DRESSED UP ALL SCARY...
...IT COULD BE ANYONE!
LATER, IN KOKAUA TOWN...
LET'S SPLIT UP.
HAGADA. HEEGADA. HOGADA.
SPLITTING UP MEANS YOU GO THE OTHER WAY. YOU'RE NOT AFRAID, ARE YOU?
HMMPH!

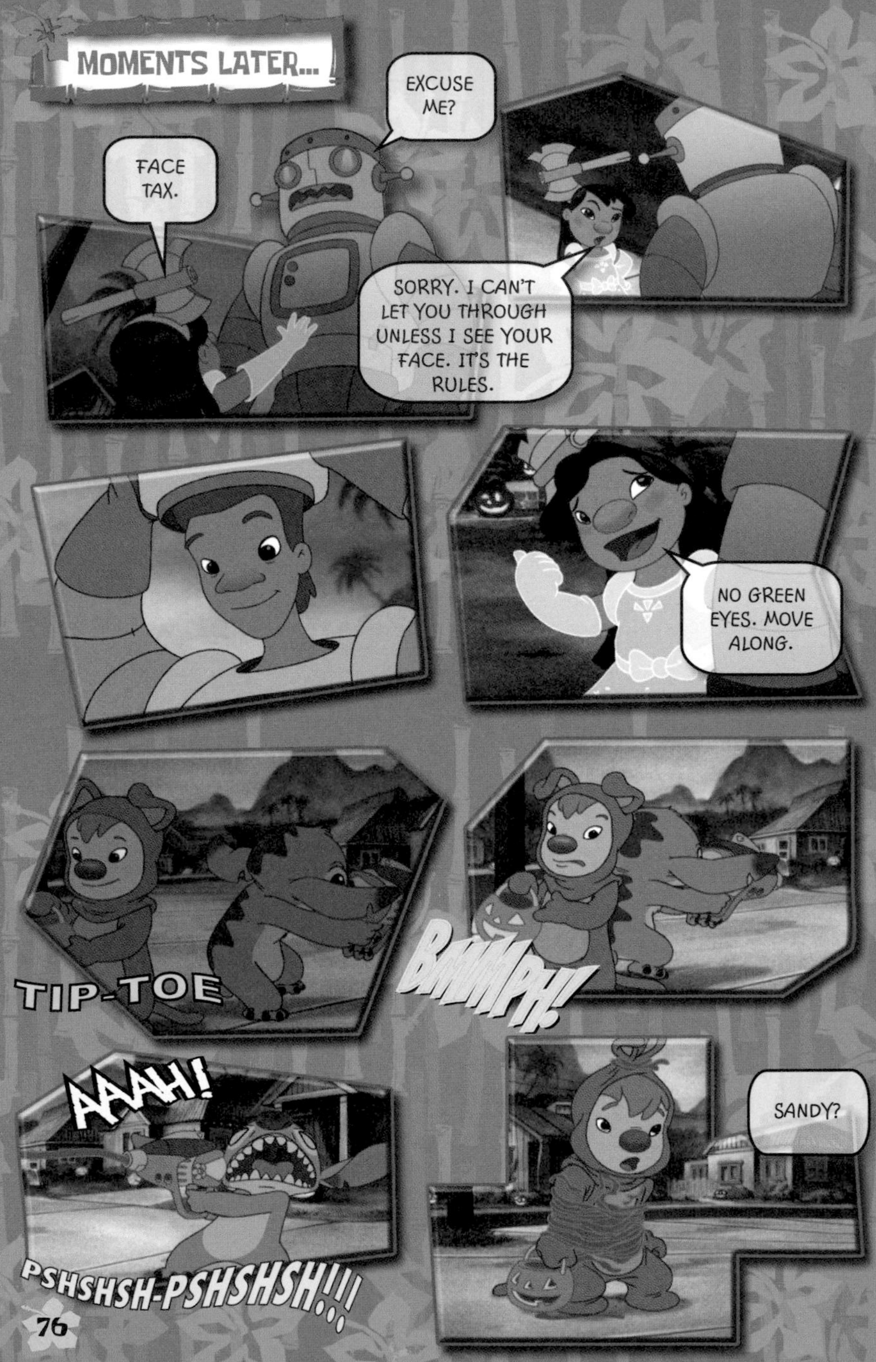
MOMENTS LATER...
FACE TAX.
EXCUSE ME?
SORRY. I CAN'T LET YOU THROUGH UNLESS I SEE YOUR FACE. IT'S THE RULES.
NO GREEN EYES. MOVE ALONG.
TIP-TOE
BRUMPH!
AAAH!
PSHSHSH-PSHSHSH!!!
SANDY?

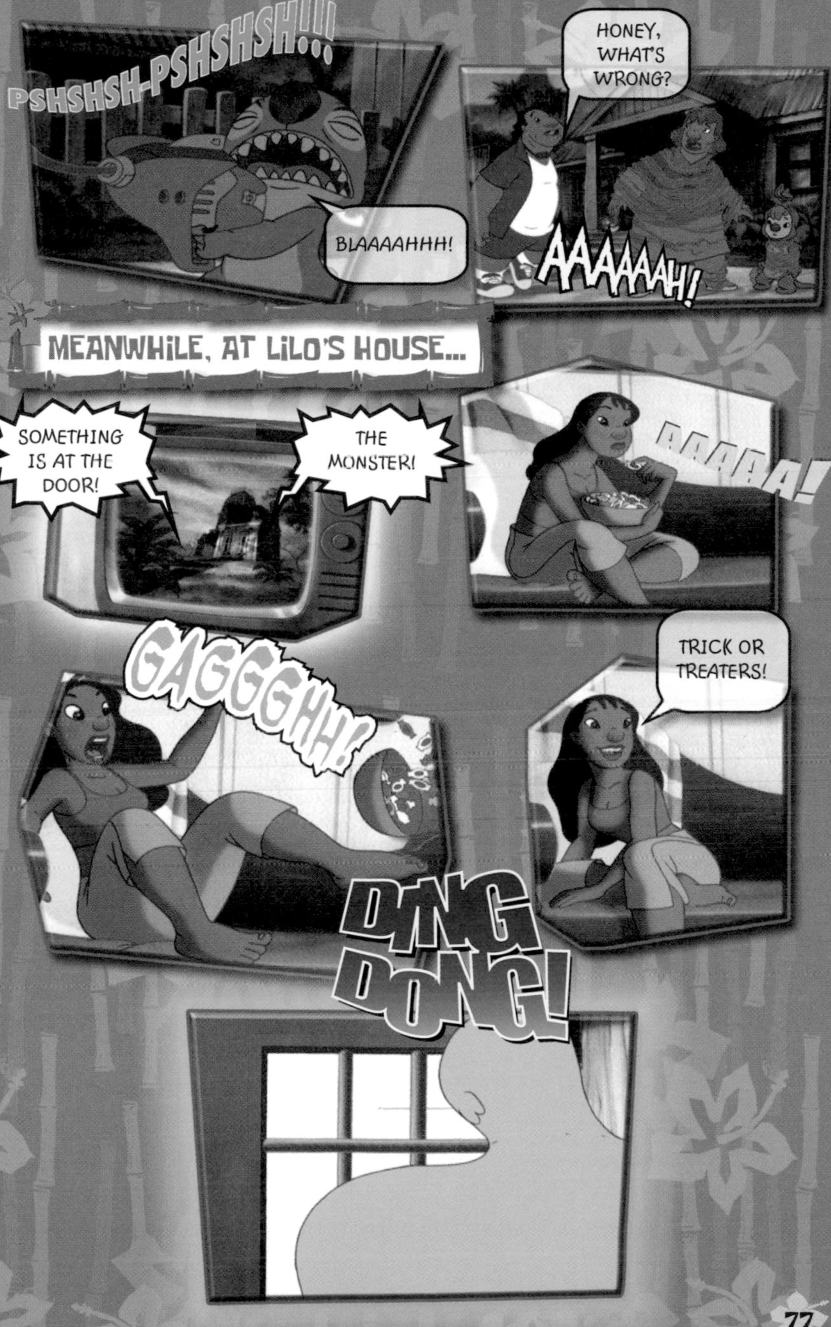

PSHSHSH-PSHSHSH!!!
BLAAAAHHH!
HONEY, WHAT'S WRONG?
AAAAAAH!
MEANWHILE, AT LILO'S HOUSE...
SOMETHING IS AT THE DOOR!
THE MONSTER!
AAAAA!
GAGGGHH!
TRICK OR TREATERS!
DING DONG!

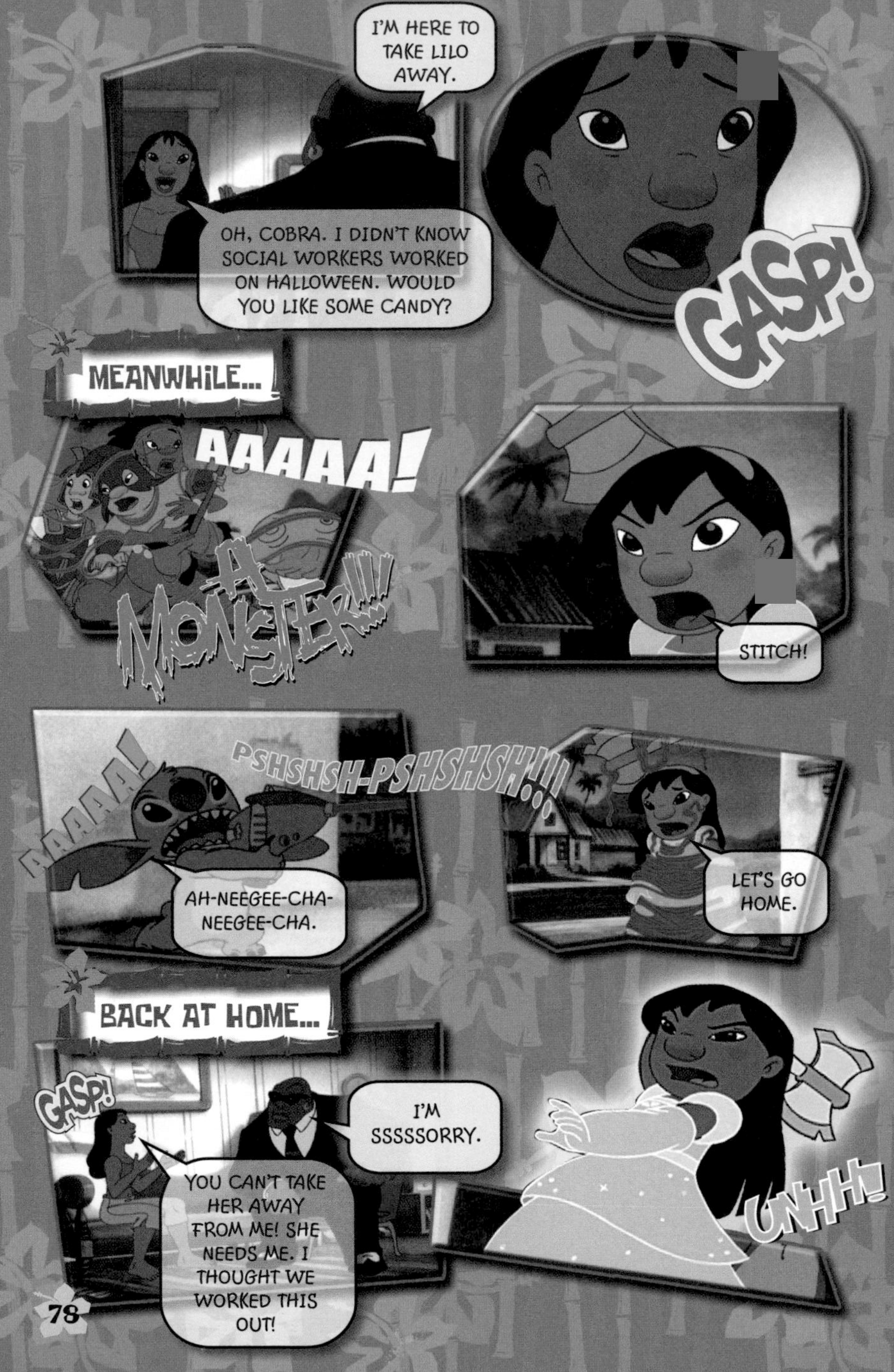
I'M HERE TO TAKE LILO AWAY.
OH, COBRA. I DIDN'T KNOW SOCIAL WORKERS WORKED ON HALLOWEEN. WOULD YOU LIKE SOME CANDY?
GASP!
MEANWHILE...
AAAAA!
A MONSTER!!!
STITCH!
AAAAA!
PSHSHSH-PSHSHSH!!!
AH-NEEGEE-CHA-NEEGEE-CHA.
LET'S GO HOME.
BACK AT HOME...
GASP!
I'M SSSSSORRY.
YOU CAN'T TAKE HER AWAY FROM ME! SHE NEEDS ME. I THOUGHT WE WORKED THIS OUT!
UNHH!

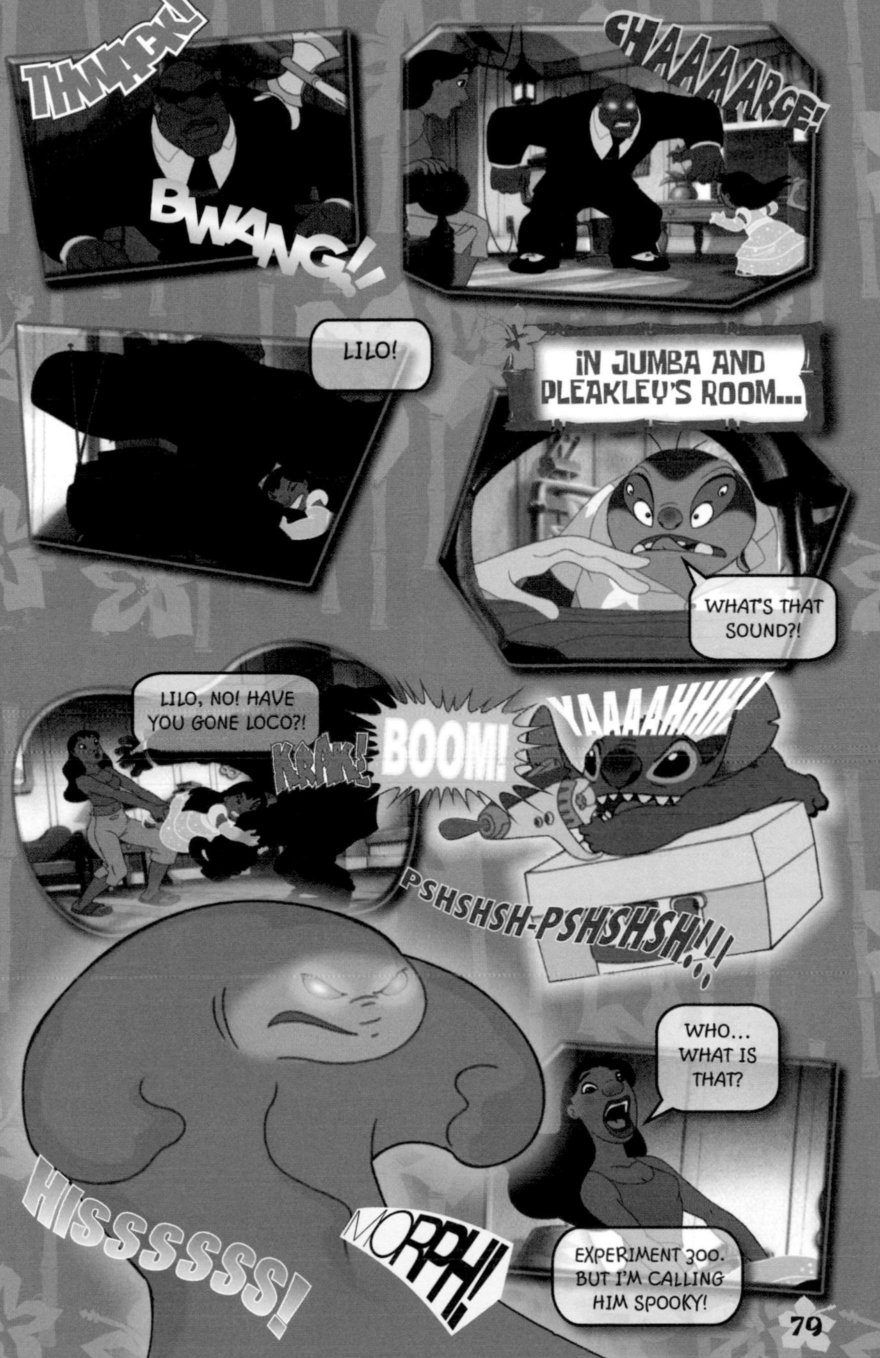
THWACK!
BWANG!!
CHAAAAARGE!
LILO!
IN JUMBA AND PLEAKLEY'S ROOM...
WHAT'S THAT SOUND?!
LILO, NO! HAVE YOU GONE LOCO?!
KRAK!
BOOM!
YAAAAHHH!
PSHSHSH-PSHSHSH!!!
WHO... WHAT IS THAT?
HISSSSSS!
MORPH!
EXPERIMENT 300. BUT I'M CALLING HIM SPOOKY!

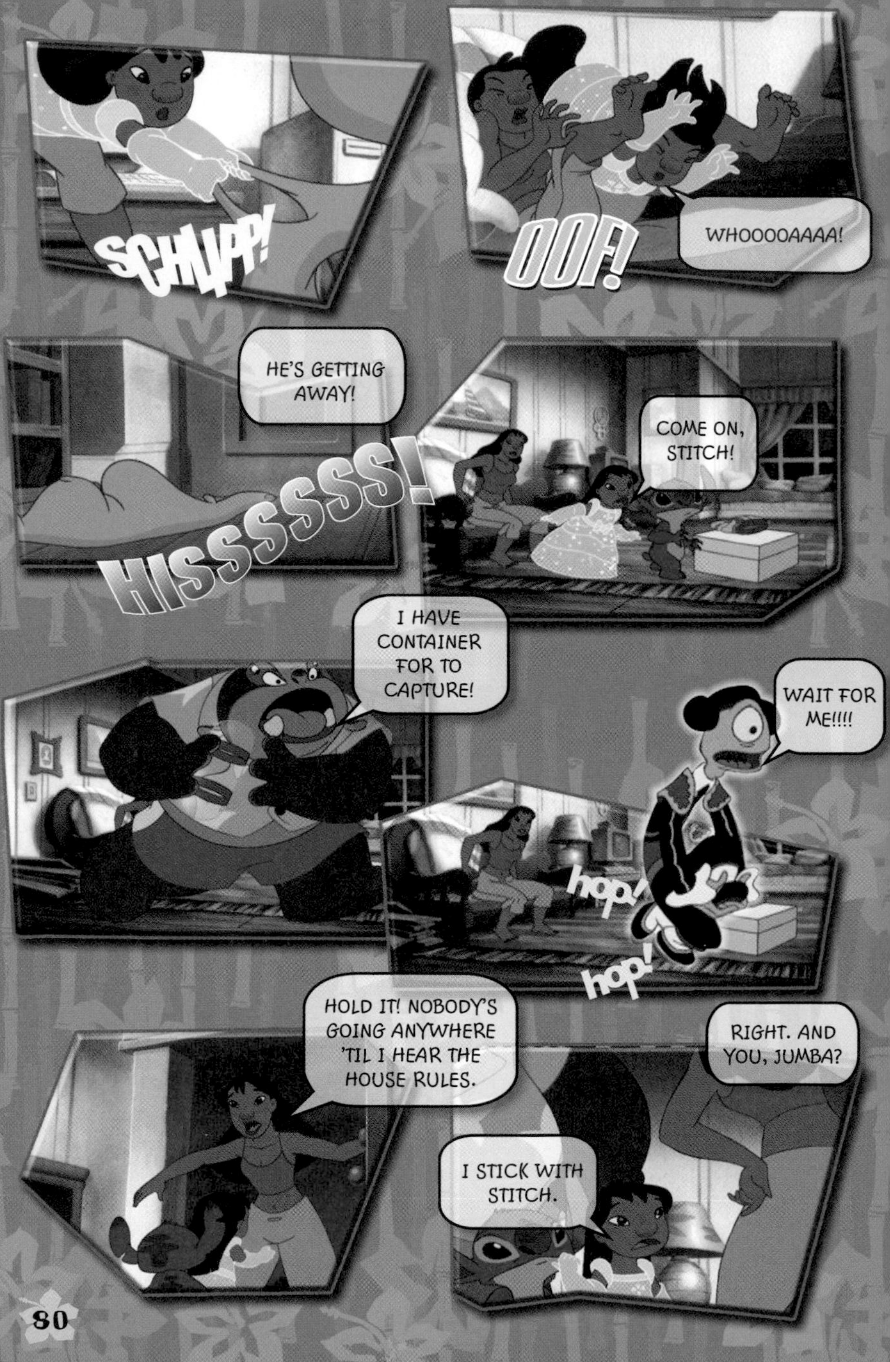
SCHUPP!
OOF!
WHOOOOAAAA!
HE'S GETTING AWAY!
HISSSSSS!
COME ON, STITCH!
I HAVE CONTAINER FOR TO CAPTURE!
WAIT FOR ME!!!!
hop!
hop!
HOLD IT! NOBODY'S GOING ANYWHERE 'TIL I HEAR THE HOUSE RULES.
RIGHT. AND YOU, JUMBA?
I STICK WITH STITCH.

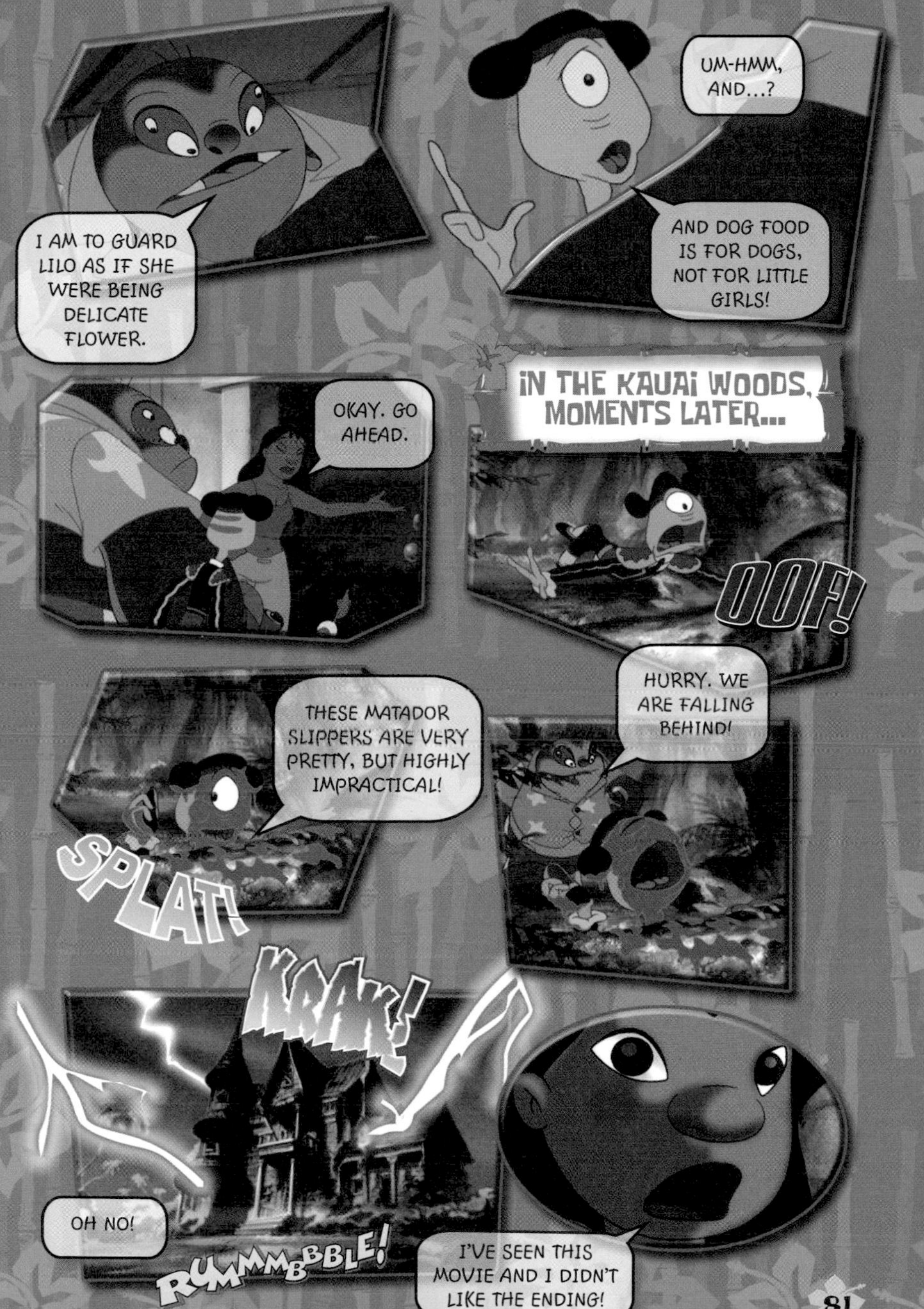
I AM TO GUARD LILO AS IF SHE WERE BEING DELICATE FLOWER.
UM-HMM, AND...?
AND DOG FOOD IS FOR DOGS, NOT FOR LITTLE GIRLS!
OKAY. GO AHEAD.
IN THE KAUAI WOODS, MOMENTS LATER...
OOF!
THESE MATADOR SLIPPERS ARE VERY PRETTY, BUT HIGHLY IMPRACTICAL!
SPLAT!
HURRY. WE ARE FALLING BEHIND!
KRAK!
OH NO!
RUMMMMBBBLE!
I'VE SEEN THIS MOVIE AND I DIDN'T LIKE THE ENDING!

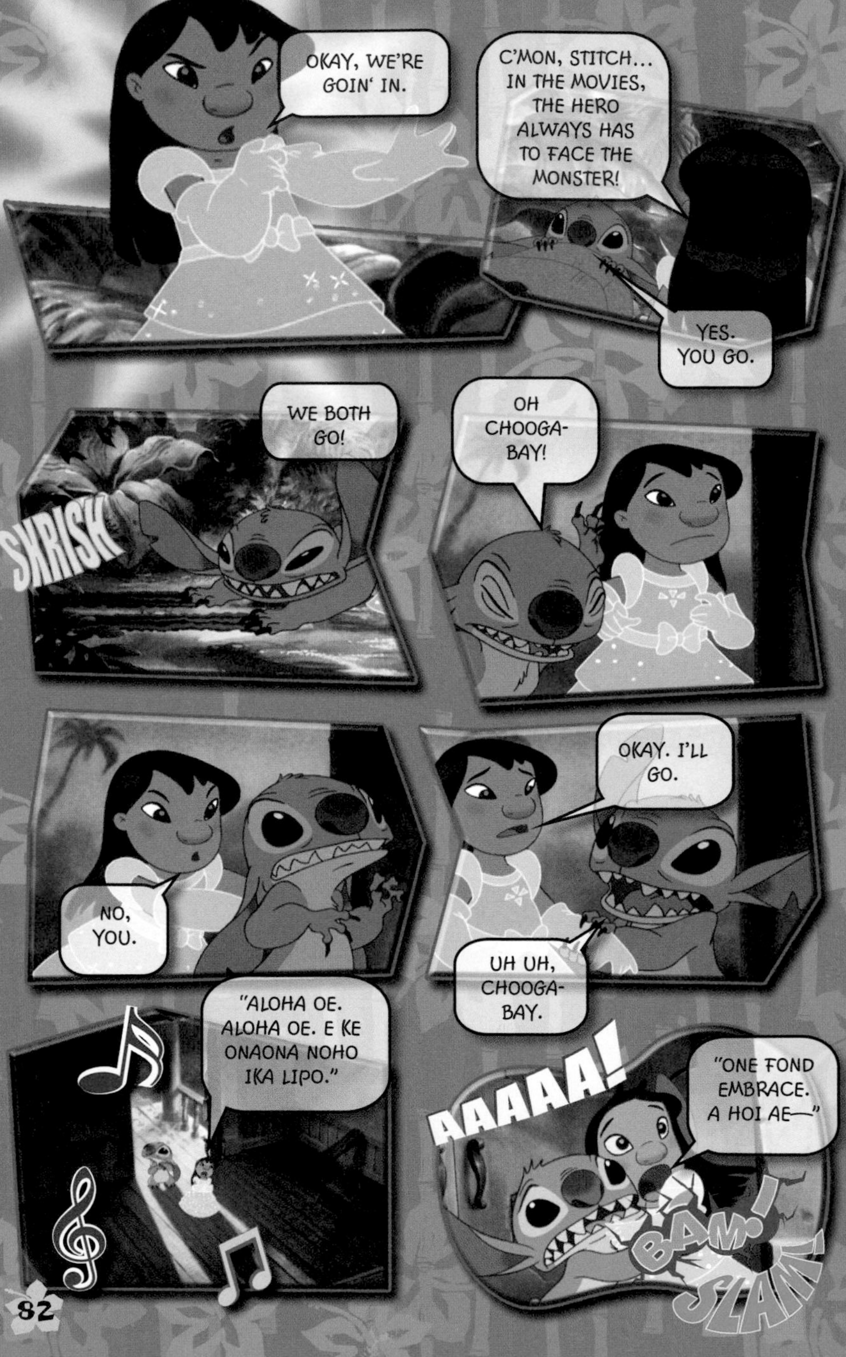
OKAY, WE'RE GOIN' IN.
C'MON, STITCH... IN THE MOVIES, THE HERO ALWAYS HAS TO FACE THE MONSTER!
YES. YOU GO.
SKRISH
WE BOTH GO!
OH CHOOGA-BAY!
NO, YOU.
OKAY. I'LL GO.
UH UH, CHOOGA-BAY.
"ALOHA OE. ALOHA OE. E KE ONAONA NOHO IKA LIPO."
AAAAA!
"ONE FOND EMBRACE. A HOI AE—"
BAM!
SLAM!

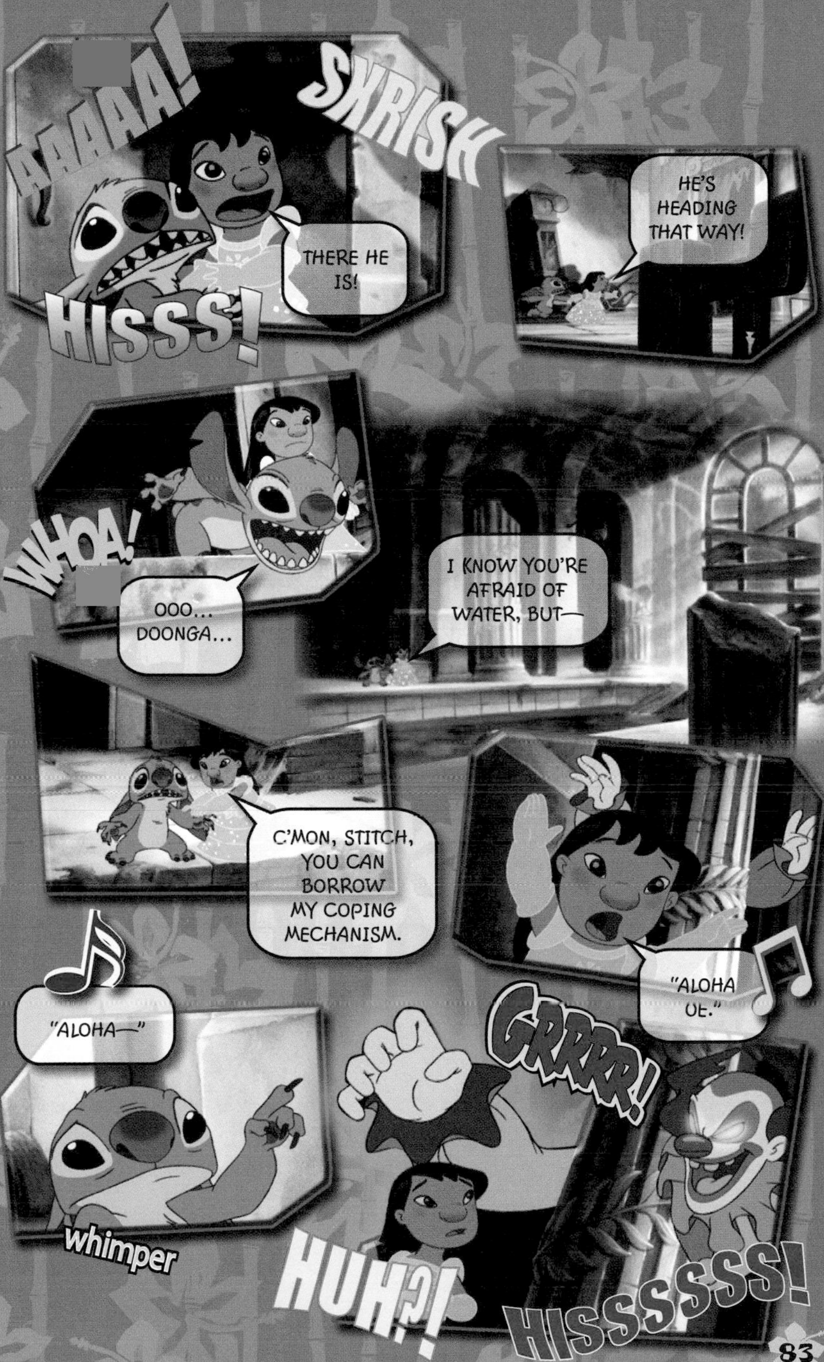
AAAAA!
SKRISH
HISSS!
THERE HE IS!
HE'S HEADING THAT WAY!
WHOA!
OOO... DOONGA...
I KNOW YOU'RE AFRAID OF WATER, BUT—
C'MON, STITCH, YOU CAN BORROW MY COPING MECHANISM.
"ALOHA OE."
"ALOHA—"
whimper
GRRRR!
HUH?!
HISSSSSS!

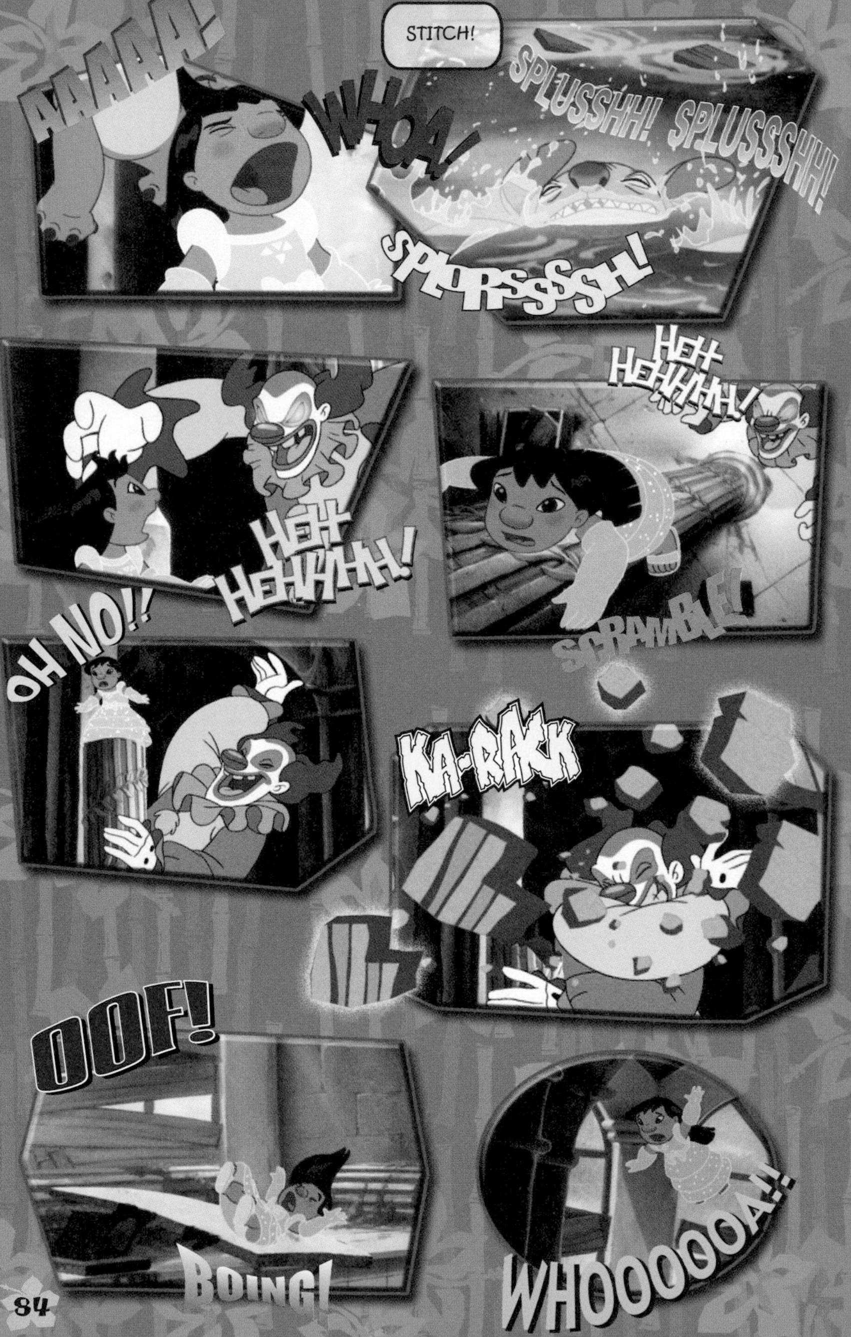

AAAAA!
STITCH!
WHOA!
SPLUSSHH! SPLUSSSHH!
SPLORSSSSH!
HEH HEHHHHH!
HEH HEHHHHH!
SCRAMBLE!
OH NO!!
KA-RACK
OOF!
BOING!
WHOOOOOA!!

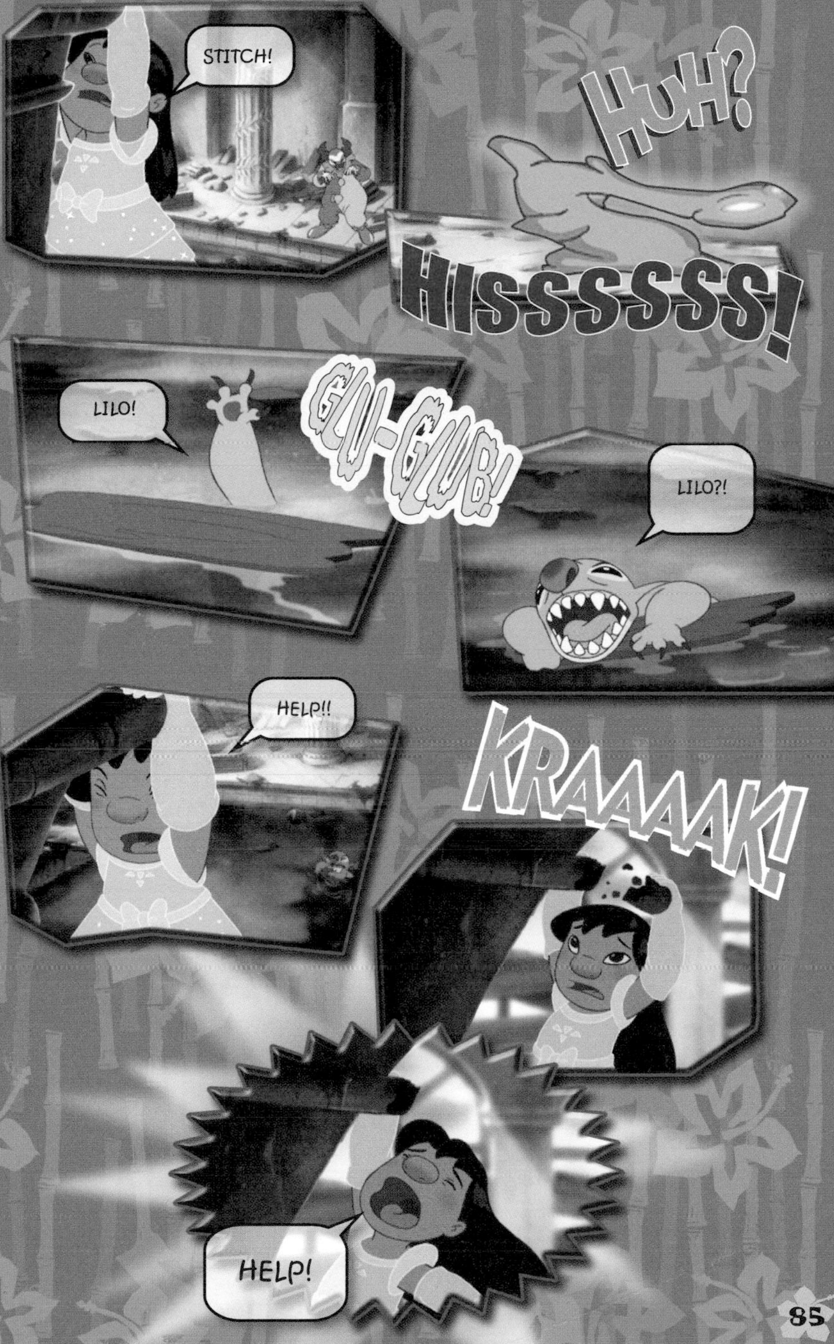
STITCH!
HUH?
HISSSSSS!
LILO!
GLU-GLUB!
LILO?!
HELP!!
KRAAAAK!
HELP!

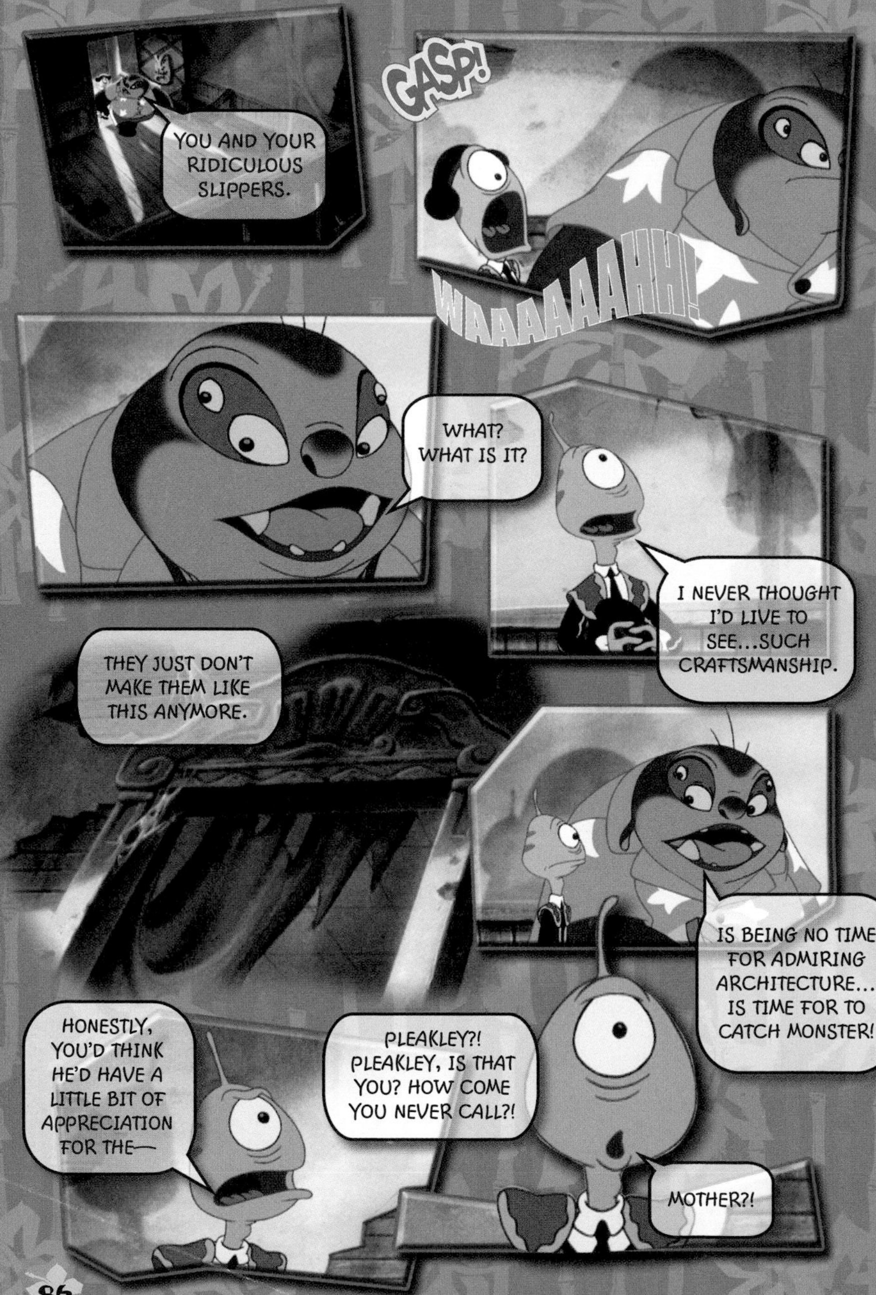
YOU AND YOUR RIDICULOUS SLIPPERS.
GASP!
WAAAAAAAHH!
WHAT? WHAT IS IT?
I NEVER THOUGHT I'D LIVE TO SEE...SUCH CRAFTSMANSHIP.
THEY JUST DON'T MAKE THEM LIKE THIS ANYMORE.
IS BEING NO TIME FOR ADMIRING ARCHITECTURE... IS TIME FOR TO CATCH MONSTER!
HONESTLY, YOU'D THINK HE'D HAVE A LITTLE BIT OF APPRECIATION FOR THE—
PLEAKLEY?! PLEAKLEY, IS THAT YOU? HOW COME YOU NEVER CALL?!
MOTHER?!

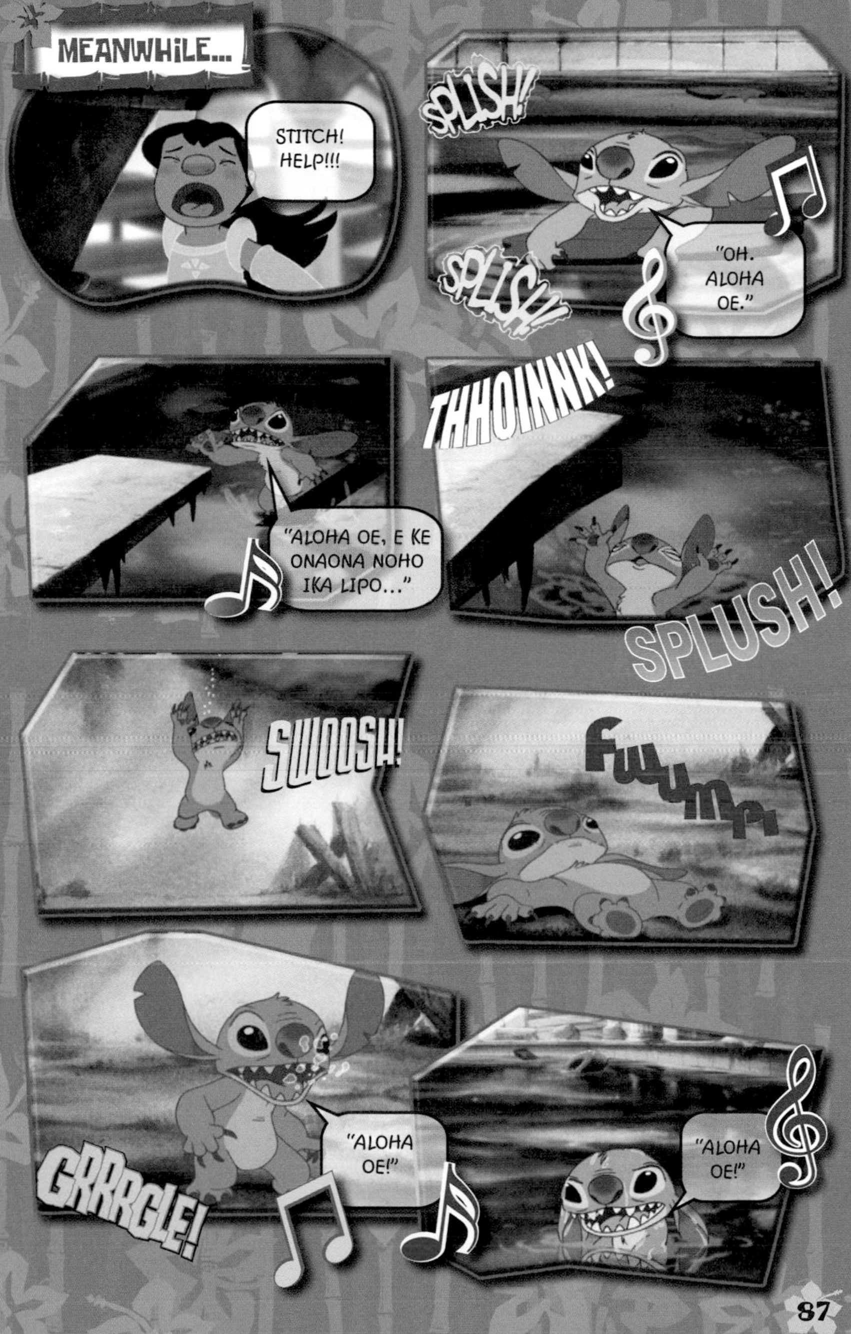
MEANWHILE...
STITCH! HELP!!!
SPLISH!
SPLISH!
"OH. ALOHA OE."
"ALOHA OE, E KE ONAONA NOHO IKA LIPO..."
THHOINNK!
SPLUSH!
SWOOSH!
FWUMP!
GRRRGLE!
"ALOHA OE!"
"ALOHA OE!"

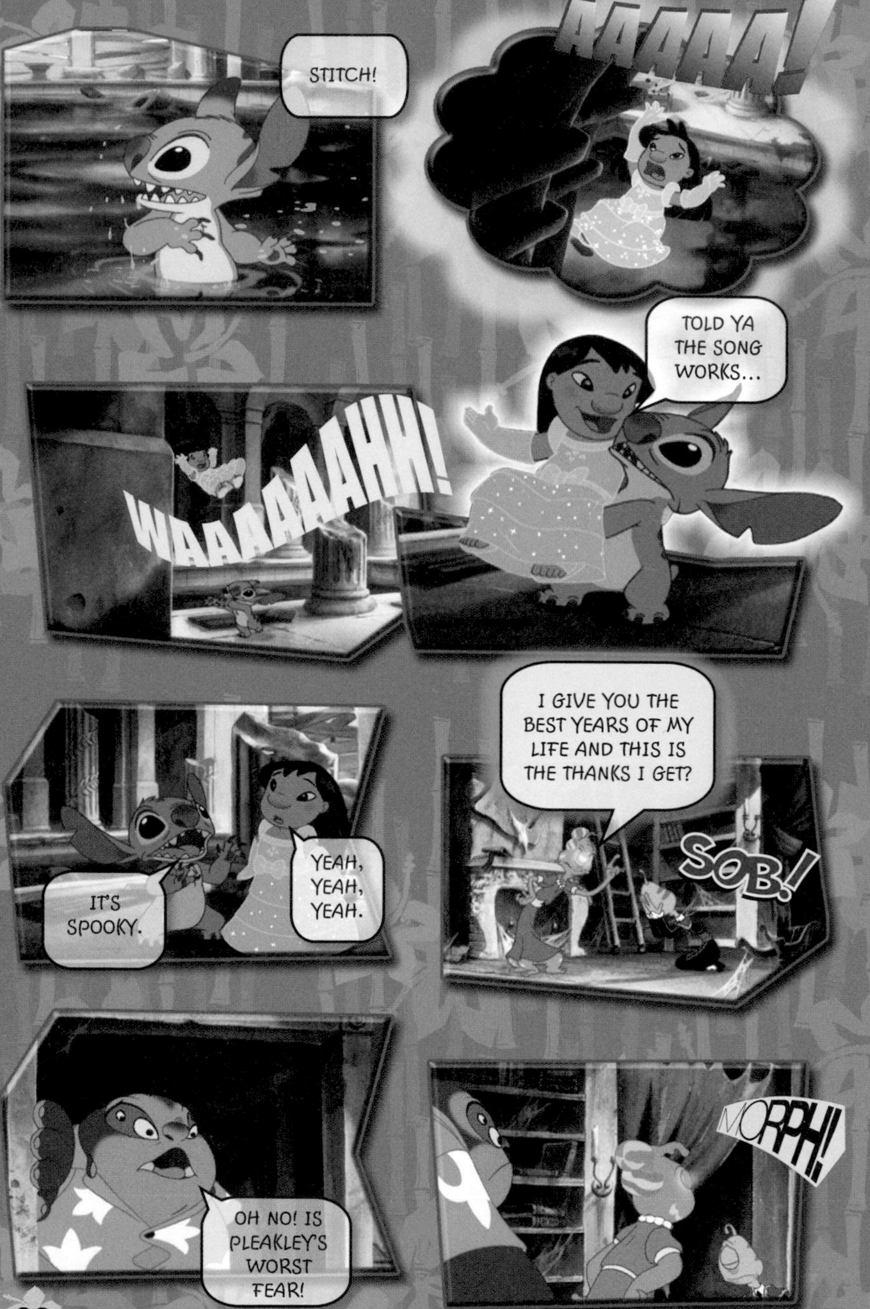
STITCH!
AAAAA!
TOLD YA THE SONG WORKS...
WAAAAAAHH!
IT'S SPOOKY.
YEAH, YEAH, YEAH.
I GIVE YOU THE BEST YEARS OF MY LIFE AND THIS IS THE THANKS I GET?
SOB!
OH NO! IS PLEAKLEY'S WORST FEAR!
MORPH!

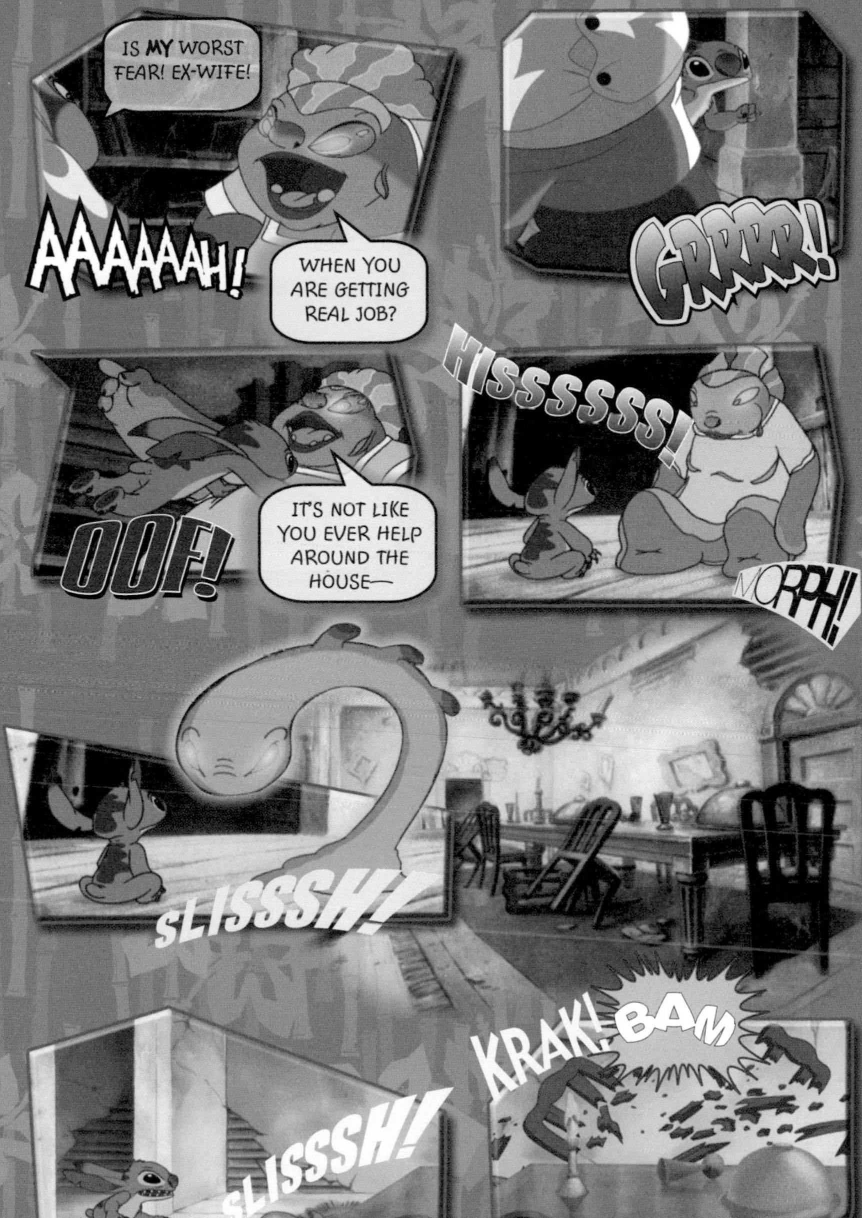

IS MY WORST FEAR! EX-WIFE!
AAAAAAAH!
WHEN YOU ARE GETTING REAL JOB?
GRRRR!
OOF!
IT'S NOT LIKE YOU EVER HELP AROUND THE HOUSE—
HISSSSSSS!
MORPH!
SLISSSH!
SLISSSH!
KRAK!
BAM

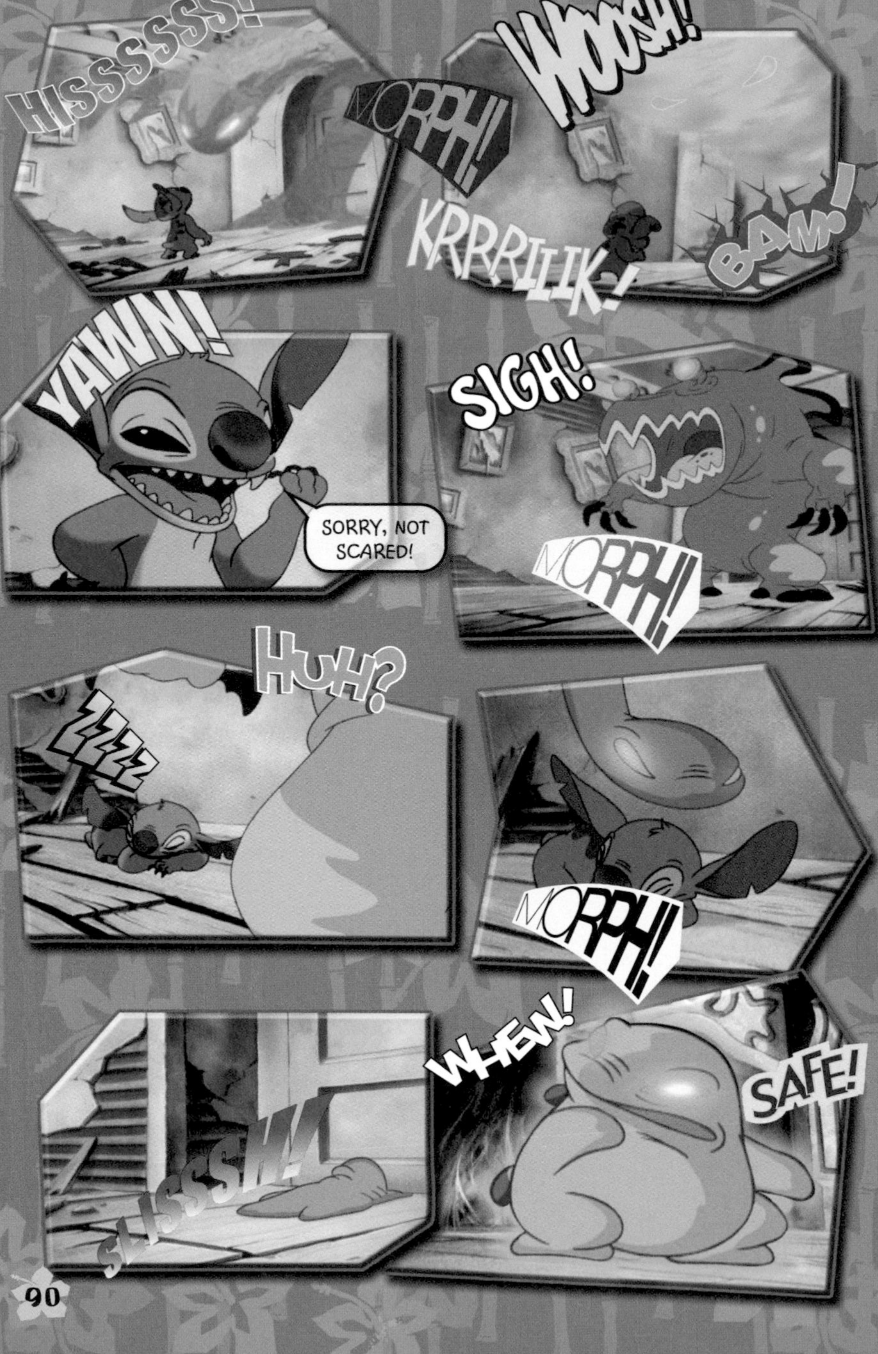
HISSSSSS!
MORPH!
WOOSH!
KRRRIIIK!
BAM!
YAWN!
SORRY, NOT SCARED!
SIGH!
MORPH!
ZZZZ
HUH?
MORPH!
SLISSSH!
WHEW!
SAFE!

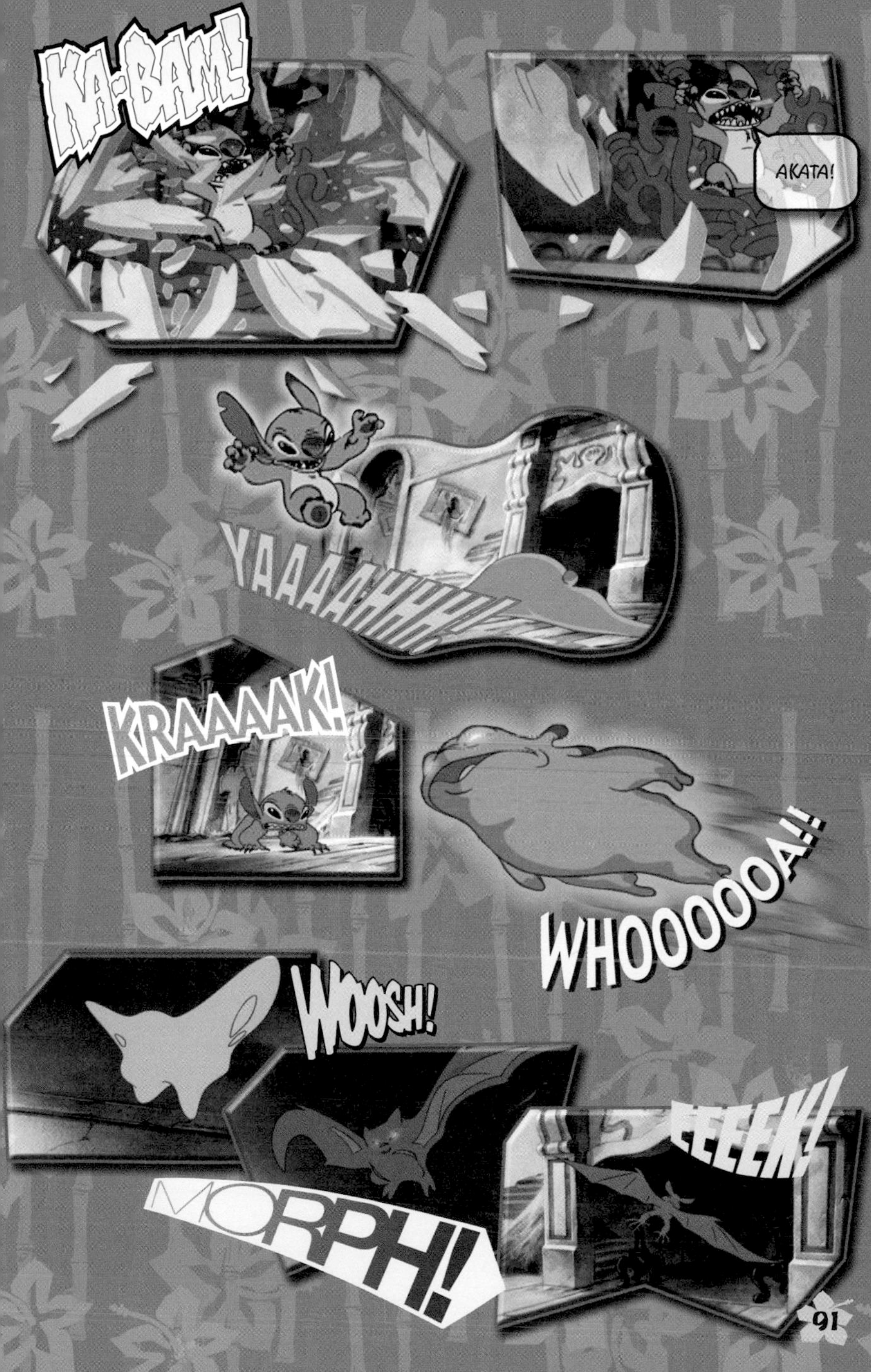
KA-BAM!
AKATA!
YAAAAHHH!
KRAAAAK!
WHOOOOOA!!
WOOSH!
MORPH!
EEEEK!

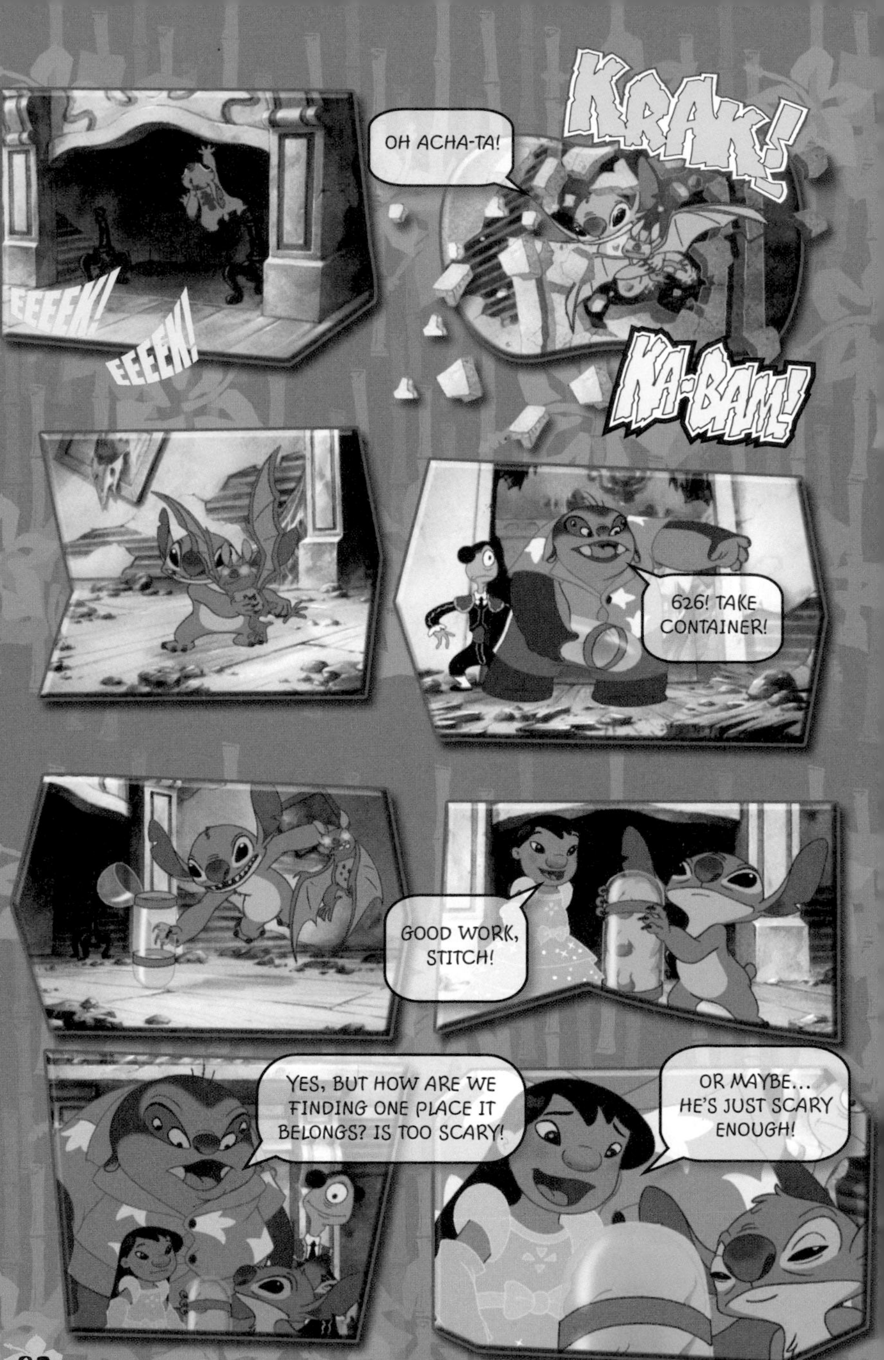
EEEEK!
EEEEK!
OH ACHA-TA!
KRAK!
KA-BAM!
626! TAKE CONTAINER!
GOOD WORK, STITCH!
YES, BUT HOW ARE WE FINDING ONE PLACE IT BELONGS? IS TOO SCARY!
OR MAYBE... HE'S JUST SCARY ENOUGH!

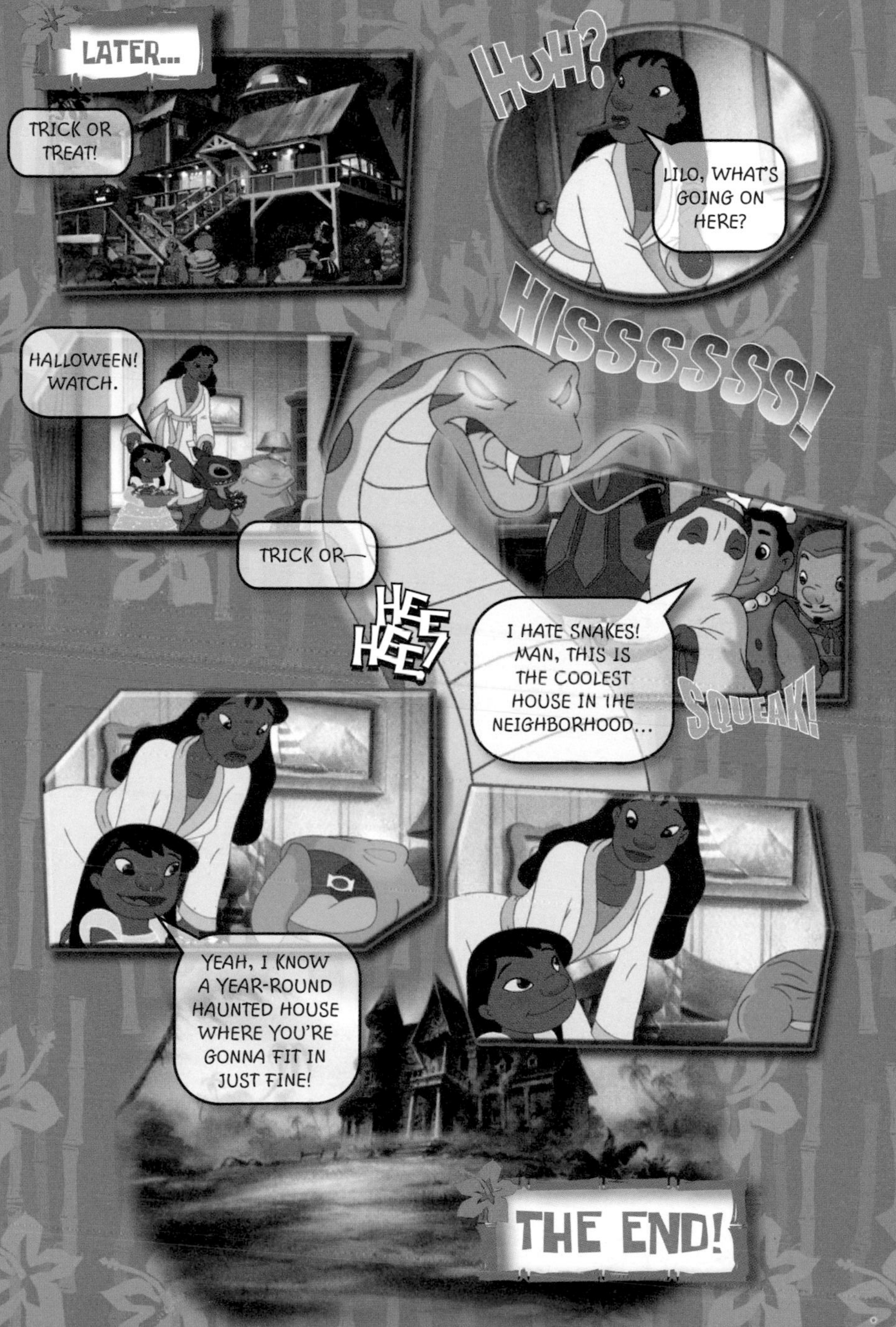
LATER...
TRICK OR TREAT!
HUH?
LILO, WHAT'S GOING ON HERE?
HALLOWEEN! WATCH.
HISSSSSSS!
TRICK OR—
HEE HEE!
I HATE SNAKES! MAN, THIS IS THE COOLEST HOUSE IN THE NEIGHBORHOOD...
SQUEAK!
YEAH, I KNOW A YEAR-ROUND HAUNTED HOUSE WHERE YOU'RE GONNA FIT IN JUST FINE!
THE END!

ALSO AVAILABLE FROM TOKYOPOP®

MANGA

.HACK//LEGEND OF THE TWILIGHT
ANGELIC LAYER
BABY BIRTH
BRAIN POWERED
BRIGADOON
B'TX
CANDIDATE FOR GODDESS, THE
CARDCAPTOR SAKURA
CARDCAPTOR SAKURA - MASTER OF THE CLOW
CHRONICLES OF THE CURSED SWORD
CLAMP SCHOOL DETECTIVES
CLOVER
COMIC PARTY
CORRECTOR YUI
COWBOY BEBOP
COWBOY BEBOP: SHOOTING STAR
CRAZY LOVE STORY
CRESCENT MOON
CULDCEPT
CYBORG 009
D•N•ANGEL
DEMON DIARY
DEMON ORORON, THE
DIGIMON
DIGIMON TAMERS
DIGIMON ZERO TWO
DRAGON HUNTER
DRAGON KNIGHTS
DRAGON VOICE
DREAM SAGA
DUKLYON: CLAMP SCHOOL DEFENDERS
ET CETERA
ETERNITY
FAERIES' LANDING
FLCL
FORBIDDEN DANCE
FRUITS BASKET
G GUNDAM
GATEKEEPERS
GIRL GOT GAME
GUNDAM BLUE DESTINY
GUNDAM SEED ASTRAY
GUNDAM WING
GUNDAM WING: BATTLEFIELD OF PACIFISTS
GUNDAM WING: ENDLESS WALTZ

GUNDAM WING: THE LAST OUTPOST (G-UNIT)
HANDS OFF!
HARLEM BEAT
IMMORTAL RAIN
I.N.V.U.
INITIAL D
INSTANT TEEN: JUST ADD NUTS
JING: KING OF BANDITS
JING: KING OF BANDITS - TWILIGHT TALES
JULINE
KARE KANO
KILL ME, KISS ME
KINDAICHI CASE FILES, THE
KING OF HELL
KODOCHA: SANA'S STAGE
LEGEND OF CHUN HYANG, THE
MAGIC KNIGHT RAYEARTH I
MAGIC KNIGHT RAYEARTH II
MAN OF MANY FACES
MARMALADE BOY
MARS
MARS: HORSE WITH NO NAME
METROID
MINK
MIRACLE GIRLS
MODEL
ONE
ONE I LOVE, THE
PEACH GIRL
PEACH GIRL: CHANGE OF HEART
PITA-TEN
PLANET LADDER
PLANETES
PRINCESS AI
PSYCHIC ACADEMY
RAGNAROK
RAVE MASTER
REALITY CHECK
REBIRTH
REBOUND
RISING STARS OF MANGA
SAILOR MOON
SAINT TAIL
SAMURAI GIRL REAL BOUT HIGH SCHOOL
SEIKAI TRILOGY, THE
SGT. FROG
SHAOLIN SISTERS

03.03.04Y

ALSO AVAILABLE FROM TOKYOPOP®

**For more
information visit
www.TOKYOPOP.com**

03.03.04Y